S0-AZT-591

Weathering Winter

A BUR OAK ORIGINAL

Weathering

A GARDENER'S DAYBOOK by Carl H. Klaus

UNIVERSITY OF IOWA PRESS Iowa City

Winter

University of Iowa Press, Iowa City 52242

Printed in the United States of America
Design by Richard Hendel
http://www.uiowa.edu/~uipress

Printed on acid-free paper

Library of Congress Cataloging-in-Publication Data
Klaus, Carl H.
Weathering winter: a gardener's daybook / by Carl H. Klaus.
p. cm.—(A Bur oak original)
ISBN 0-87745-594-5 (cloth)
1. Vegetable gardening—Iowa—Iowa City—Anecdotes. 2. Gardeners—Iowa—Iowa City—Anecdotes. 3. Winter—Iowa—Iowa City—Anecdotes. 4. Klaus, Carl H.—Diaries. I. Title. II. Series.
SB320.7.I8K586 1997
635—dc21 97-5720

97 98 99 00 01 02 C 5 4 3 2

A portion of this work (February 1–February 15) was first published in the *Kansas Quarterly/Arkansas Review* 28, no. 2.

Illustrations by Claudia McGehee

TO JOHN C. GERBER

Mentor for All Seasons

One must have a mind of winter . . .

Wallace Stevens, "The Snow Man"

When winter comes heaven will

rain success on you.

Fortune cookie

CONTENTS

ACKNOWLEDGMENTS

I'm grateful to the University of Iowa for a research leave that gave me time to envision this journal and begin turning my days into a winter daybook. During the chilling months of January, February, and early March, I was warmed by the encouragement of several people who took the time to read a few weeks or an early draft of the entire season. For their thoughtful reactions, I'm grateful to Connie Brothers, Bill Bulger, Rebecca Childers, David Hamilton, Diane Horton, and Mary Swander. My special thanks to Paul Diehl, Trudy Dittmar, Charles Drum, Mary Hussmann, Dan Roche, and Jan Weissmiller for their detailed reactions to a later draft of the journal; also to the students in my graduate journal-writing course for their frank discussion of its wintry themes — Valicia Boudry, Ellen Fagg, Vanessa Jones, Dorian Karchmar, Marilyn Knight, Patricia McKinley, Judith Mitchell, Angela Morales, Shanti Roundtree, Mitra Sedehi, and Elizabeth Tsukahara.

Most of all, I am indebted to Kate Franks for keeping me accurate and in touch with the special truths of winter.

WINTER / AN INTRODUCTION

Winter. Beloved of cross-country skiers, downhill racers, ice skaters, snowballers, snowmen, and snowplow manufacturers. Also beloved of folks who live in Tampa, San Diego, Honolulu, and other tropical spots where arctic weather advisories are never heard, except as good news for the tourist trade. But for most people who live in the temperate zone, winter is a time of plummeting temperatures, soaring heat bills, freezing rain, stalled cars, frozen pipes, and frigid ground. The season from hell, where beneath the fires in Dante's inferno, lies the ninth circle, the lowest level, the place of eternally freezing cold. No wonder so many people have moved from the Snowbelt deep into the Sunbelt, where the ground never freezes and the year never dies. Where the gardening season and the homegrown vegetables never end. I too have thought from time to time about making the move, especially when I've been walking the four-mile stretch of beach along Hanelei Bay on the north shore of Kauai in late December or early January. The sand under my feet, the sun on my cheek, Kate by my side, and the mild Pacific air all around me in a warm embrace. I've even gone so far as to thumb through real estate ads for beachfront homes along that fabled bay, where *South Pacific* was filmed and Bali Hai is forever visible in the middle distance of one's mind. But soon enough reality takes hold again, and not just in the form of real estate prices far beyond my pocket book, but also in the haunting voice that rises within me, sounding its strange refrain—"But how about winter? How about winter? Could you really give it up forever?" Then I know that winter is deep within my bones, from sixty-five years of weathering its cold embrace in places like Ohio, Michigan, New York, Maine, and Iowa.

But why the winter holds me and how I make it through—those are questions I never before tried to answer except in the pages of a daily journal I kept during the winter of 1994–95. This daybook takes stock of things in and around the nineteenth-century brick home in Iowa City where Kate and I have been tending our gardens, our pets, and ourselves for the past twenty-seven years, savoring the vegetables, herbs, and fruit that we grow on our three-quarter-acre lot, and trying to get on peaceably with the other creatures who live off the land. So this journal is, in one sense, a companion to *My Vegetable Love*, the daybook I kept during the spring, summer, and fall of 1995. Especially given its focus on our daily adventures in living close to the land, close to the bone, and close to the dining-room table.

But in another sense, this daybook covers new ground in its single-minded devotion to winter, the one season that does not make an appearance in *My Vegetable Love.* A season so apparently at odds with the very thought of gardening that when I started the year-long journal that eventually turned into both *Weathering Winter* and *My Vegetable Love*, some of my well-meaning friends and colleagues advised me just to skip over the winter months and get on with the growing season. They seemed to be telling me, in one way or another, that growth doesn't take place in winter, as if everything were temporarily on hold until spring, as if winter gardening were a contradiction in terms, and winter itself so forbidding a time that no one could possibly want to read about it. But I couldn't help thinking about the gardening catalogues that arrive in winter and the gardening dreams and the gardening squabbles with Kate about what to grow and where to grow it. And the snow falling, the birds flocking in, the icicles growing, the cabin fever rising, the buds swelling, and the seed trays coming to life overnight. So much to write about I could hardly resist.

Besides, I couldn't help thinking that winter, after all, makes up a quarter of the year, a quarter of our lives, and that all of us sooner or later must find a way of weathering its intimations of mortality, no matter where we live.

Weathering Winter

SATURDAY / DECEMBER 31

"I'm going out to feed the birds." And out she went, the back door and storm door clattering behind her. Kate, in her Wellington boots, corduroy pants, and my old hooded parka, traversing the same path she's been trekking the past twenty-five winters. So familiar, I can see it with my eyes closed. A brief stop on the back porch to fill the two-quart plastic cup with mixed seed, then across the limestone terrace, up the stone steps by the gazebo, up the sloping yard by the big vegetable garden, to the hundred-year-old pear tree, standing like a sentinel in the middle of our backyard, a house-shaped bird feeder dangling from its lowest branch. But if my eyes had been closed, I wouldn't have seen the snow falling this afternoon, enough already on the ground for Kate's footprints to be clearly visible from the porch to the tree and then back again to fill the feeder a few feet beyond our kitchen window. Eyes closed or open, though, I certainly would have heard the urgency in her voice. I've heard that terse announcement about going to feed the birds so many times that I know it's not just a statement about going to feed the birds. It's really about the weather turning bad, the birds in trouble, or, in this case, winter finally having arrived after an incredibly long-drawn-out fall. So warm a week ago that for Christmas Eve dinner, Kate made a purée of leek and potato soup with fresh leeks from our garden, as well as Russian borscht with fresh beets from our garden. Tonight, by contrast, the only homegrown stuff was some fresh parsley I harvested from under the row covers. I wish we also had some of our own French chives from the herb bed to mince up with the parsley and mix in with the grated garlic and the cracker crumbs and the olive oil and the lemon juice for topping the quick-baked oysters on the half shell. But when Kate and I were sitting across from each other at her candlelit table, sipping our champagne and eating our traditional New Year's Eve dinner of baked oysters, I could hardly tell the difference between our homegrown chives and the store-bought scallions I used instead. I could tell the difference between the store-bought endive and our delicate frisée that was frozen out by a brief cold snap in early December. But the peeled fresh grapefruit sections and the pomegranate seeds and the celery seed dressing on top of the greens were so piquant that the difference hardly mattered, especially after a few glasses of champagne and a few hearty toasts to the new year and the snow and the advent of winter.

SUNDAY / JANUARY 1

New Year's day and a newly fallen snow, completely covering the ground. So pristine in the early morning sun it makes me wonder why no one ever sings about dreaming of a white new year. A fresh start. Last year's leavings so well hidden, it's momentarily hard for me to believe how green things were just a week ago. And warm enough too on Christmas day that I was walking around outside in just a shirt and a lightweight sweater. And so were my daughter Hannah and my son-in-law, Monty, and my grandchildren, Ben and Lizzie, visiting from California. Actually, it almost felt as if I were in California rather than here in Iowa. And well I might have been, given the radishes and turnips I was harvesting, thanks to the warmth of the fall and my spunbond, polyester row covers. But now, all the marks of that day are gone. Hannah and Monty back in California. The radishes and turnips eaten, row covers put away, the soil turned and completely covered with a different kind of white. The row cover of winter.

Still, the snowcover's not so thick that I can't see the rolls and ripples of the land beneath it. Especially when I'm looking down on it from my big windows up here in our attic study. The outlines of the garden beds are also visible from here. And the heavings of the turned soil in the beds. And the remnants of Kate's footprints back and forth to the bird feeder in the pear tree. The snow turns the landscape into a memory of itself, selectively marking the comings and goings, the doings and undoings that have taken place on it during the past several months, or weeks, or days, or hours. Preserving the rabbit tracks and deer tracks of the predawn morning. Concealing the frozen shreds of lettuce and leek at the newly turned end of the vegetable garden.

But there's nothing like getting outside to take the measure of things — or have them take the measure of you. Before going for a walk with Kate in midafternoon, I thought the wind was relatively light. Just a slight swing of the feeder in the pear tree and a faint rustle of dried clematis at the end of the gazebo. Nothing to worry about. But we weren't out more than a minute or two when Kate, who doesn't ordinarily fret about such things, announced matter-of-factly, "The wind is sharp." And a few minutes later, "It's steady on." And a few minutes later, "There's ice in it." Sometimes winter is best in small doses, especially at first. So we headed back home again, where I checked the Weather Channel and discovered that the temperature was eleven degrees above with the wind blowing at sixteen miles an hour to produce a windchill factor of seventeen degrees below. No more dreaming of a white new year. I'm still remembering a green Christmas.

MONDAY / JANUARY 2

A week ago the weather was so balmy that the pussy willows at the back of the yard were beginning to open, and I was thinking about planting a few radish seeds in the back vegetable bed, where I'd just finished harvesting the last of the turnips. But today it probably won't get above twenty, tonight it's supposed to hit ten or fifteen below zero, and a bitter cold spell is predicted to hang on for the next several days.

So now I'm wondering how I could ever have been beguiled into thinking I could bring on another crop of radishes under the row covers. You'd think that thirty-two years of living in Iowa would have convinced me that winter in the upper Midwest inevitably delivers at least one arctic cold spell, usually more, usually in January, and the sun never gets high enough in the sky to deliver the necessary light and heat for a crop of radishes or anything else. But even Kate, who was born and raised just twenty miles north of here, who knows the seasonal truths far better than I—even Kate thought it might be worth trying a few radish seeds. What is it, I wonder, that leads us to suppose a pleasant quirk in the weather might turn into a long run of balmy days? The power of suggestion? The dread of winter and of wintry reflections? The yearning for spring? The hunger for spring radishes? Or just the force of the moment itself and all its pleasing sensations—the gentleness of the air, the warmth of the sun, the feel of the soil, the delicate taste of the row-covered spinach that made it through the early December cold snap?

Whatever the case, I'm now wondering if the spinach will survive this harsh cold spell. But then again, if the row-covered parsley made it through last year's bitter January, why not the spinach? And the late-planted shallot bulbs? And the row-covered thyme on the south end of the gazebo? And the pair of artichoke plants too? After all, nothing is certain here except death, taxes, and a January cold snap.

TUESDAY / JANUARY 3

By this point in the winter, my bodily thermometer is usually so well calibrated that it comes within a few degrees of the weather reports. But the drop this year has been so sudden that I'm not yet capable of accurately feeling the difference between seven above, as it was this morning, and seven below, which was more what it felt like, probably because the windchill then was eighteen below. Sometimes, I wonder if I'll also get attuned to the onset of the mortal chill, so I can track its progress as calmly as the falling temperature.

I'm not yet adjusted to the cost of the store-bought vegetables either, as I discovered from a trip to the local supermarket this afternoon. Just a month or so ago, we were still eating the last of the fresh peppers I'd harvested from the garden in early November. But now, a medium-sized green pepper with a few telltale wrinkles on its shoulders cost me 89 cents. And the lettuce situation is even more disturbing, especially when I think about all the greens I was gradually harvesting just a few weeks ago—buttercrunch heads, green leaf, purple oak leaf, arugula, and endive, all flourishing under row covers until the night of December 10, when the temperature plunged below zero, froze all the greens, and then just as quickly warmed up again, as if to taunt me for hoarding all my produce under row covers. Now, the spray-soaked stuff at the supermarket is selling for $1.89 a pound.

During my Depression-era childhood in Cleveland, Ohio, one couldn't get fresh peppers or lettuce in January for any amount of money. So perhaps I shouldn't be complaining about the cost of supermarket produce. Maybe I should be celebrating the elaborate national and international network of growers and wholesalers and refrigeraters and shippers and merchandisers that make it possible for me to buy a green pepper to put in the creole baked snapper I'm planning to cook this evening. But then again, there's a part of me that likes to get my produce closer to home. So, after all, the most tasty and satisfying parts of the baked snapper will be our homegrown, home-canned tomatoes that I fetch up from the basement and the fresh thyme I've already harvested from the row-covered herbs at the end of the gazebo. When I brought the thyme clippings into the house, they smelled as dusky and rank as if it were still midsummer — and it still was, at least in my nose, at least for a moment.

❧ ❧

WEDNESDAY / JANUARY 4

"Seven below," said my nose to me when I stepped outside to get the morning paper, and this time the sensation was so strong — the air in my nostrils so harsh — I was certain of being close to the mark. This time, in fact, I was right on the mark. So were my gloveless fingers, screeching a windchill of twenty-seven below. Now that my bodily gauges seem to be working, I needn't rely on the weather reports or our outdoor thermometer. All I need do is consult my internal thermometer. Or look at the signs all around me. The woodpeckers and starlings squabbling for time at the suet feeder. The sparrows congregating at the seed tray. The surface of the lily pond frozen, except for a slight hole made by the stocktank heater, to help winter over the goldfish. Our Welsh terrier, Pip, scratching to get in just a few minutes after asking to be let out. Our foundling cat, Phoebe, not even asking to be let out. And water sitting in the sink of the downstairs bathroom, evidence that the drainage pipe below had frozen overnight. All the instruments agree that this is the coldest one yet.

Time to put on my long johns, plug in the car, hunker down inside, and wonder, as I always do, how bad it might get before it's all over. Is this the cold wave, the winter storm, that'll outfreeze the worst one I can remember? It swept through here in January 1979, with fifteen inches of snow, then a temperature drop to thirty below and winds gusting up to sixty miles an hour — on a weekend when Kate and I had planned a party to welcome twenty professors from around the country, some of them coming from places as warm as Alabama, California, and Hawaii, to spend six months at an institute on writing that I was directing here in Iowa City. Some welcome! But the thing I remember more than the paralyzing storm was the eagerness it aroused in everyone to brave the elements, to make it here, even at the risk of driving several hundred miles through back roads and closed highways in a ramshackle old Cadillac, as one fellow did coming from Pennsylvania. And then trudging up to our house through waist-high trenches of snow.

I've never been quite so reckless a pioneer, but ever since then I've noticed that winter rouses in me both a sense of menace and a sense of challenge — the haunting look of a dead man's hands that comes whenever my fingers turn white and painful at the slightest exposure to freezing temperatures (Raynaud's syndrome, according to the doctor), and yet my irrepressible desire to confront the worst that nature can throw my way (especially in the comfort of a centrally heated nineteenth-century brick home). Maybe that's what lures me downstairs on days like this to the Plexiglas-covered steps of our outside cellarway, where I winter over a bunch of warm-weather plants just a foot or so away from the bitter cold. The challenge of keeping them going from fall to spring. Bay, lemon grass, rosemary, sage, tarragon, azalea, gerbera, spider plant, and cymbidium orchid (until it's been chilled long enough to begin setting bloomstalks).

When I took up gardening some forty years ago, the season began in April and ended in October — from the end of frost to the onset of frost. But now I'm gardening nonstop from January through December, frost and freeze be damned. And I don't know how I feel about this endless growing season. On the one hand, I like to think of myself as being in tune with nature, so I'm a bit uneasy about all these Plexiglas and polyester contraptions I'm using to defy winter. But there's also a part of me, I guess, that's unwilling to accept the end of the growing season and all that it suggests about the ending of life itself. An unwillingness that puts me in mind of the winter I was nine years old and developed, seemingly out of nowhere, a deep conviction there was something so special about me that I would never die (as both of my parents had several years before). Or maybe my winter gardening is just a matter of liking homegrown produce, or liking to show I can produce it under any conditions. In every garden (and gardener), there's a snake lurking somewhere on the premises.

THURSDAY / JANUARY 5

In every gardener, there's also a dream lurking somewhere on the premises, especially during the bitterly cold days of a winter deep freeze. The dream of an early spring day that's sunny enough and warm enough to be outside in the garden. Or a dream of the first summer harvest. Or the first ripe tomato. Or the first fresh tomato sauce, redolent with the aroma of fresh chopped basil and minced garlic. And there's nothing like the arrival of the spring gardening catalogues to help the dream along, glowing with emblems of summer. A ripe tomato (or two or three) prominently in the foreground of almost every cover, like the watercolor still-life of vegetables on the Shepherd's Seed catalogue that turned up in the mailbox this afternoon. And not only some glowing red tomatoes, but also a glossy purple eggplant, a cranberry-colored head of radicchio, a bright yellow pepper sitting next to a green pepper turning red at the top of its shoulders, a couple heads of pale white garlic, a few sprigs of basil, and a big crinkly green leaf of kale, all appetizingly arrayed upon a bright blue-and-yellow-striped tablecloth. As sunny as summer itself.

As sunny as winter, too, at least for the moment. No matter how bad the temperature or the windchill gets in January, the sun seems to shine more brightly now than at any other time of the year. An illusion aided, no doubt, by its low angle in the sky and its reflection on the snow. It shines more regularly too. Five days in a row so far. The color of its reflected light and the texture of the shadows it casts on the snow change continuously, as I can see from my third-floor perspective. Early this morning at sunrise, it cast a shadowless orange aura over the backyard. A few hours later, the yard seemed bathed in a piercingly white light, broken only by the sharply defined and very dark shadows of the trees. A few hours later, the shadows began to soften and the light turned faintly yellow. And now, late in the afternoon, the shadows have completely disappeared, the snow is grayish, and soon it will change color again at the fabled blue hour.

No wonder the Scandinavians cherish the sun so much they've developed a special light bulb to compensate for the long periods when they're deprived of sunlight. I first heard about such light bulbs when I was reading the newspaper this morning, and one of them exploded in the table lamp just a few feet from my head, scattering its pale purple shards on the carpet around my feet. A few minutes later, Kate hustled downstairs to see what had happened, and it was then that she explained to me how these light bulbs are meant to "cut down on depression and lift your spirits," because, as one of the ads for them reports, "their bright, glare-free light is the closest thing to natural daylight." Natural daylight, thank God, doesn't explode just a few feet from my head, but it does lift my spirits. Even now, when its glow is barely perceptible in the snow that is so blue, so blue as to be inseparable from the sky.

FRIDAY / JANUARY 6

The snow sure stood out this morning, especially after a few more inches overnight. Not much in itself, but enough on top of the rest to make it look and feel as if we might be starting one of those long winter buildups I remember from my childhood in Cleveland, and from several years of living on the coast of Maine and in upstate New York. Deep enough almost to begin forming trenches along the shoveled sidewalks. Also enough to whiten up the animal tracks in the backyard, so they now look like ghostly impressions rather than clearcut footprints and tailprints in the snow. Along with the snow came an overcast sky and a temperature in the mid twenties. Almost warm enough to feel cozy by comparison with yesterday and the day before. And now at midday the snow is falling again, filling the sky with flakes, changing the look of things even as I try to put them into words.

Change, it seems, is at the heart of things, as I discovered anew when I took our nineteen-year-old cat, Phoebe, into the vet this morning, to check on the open sore in her hindquarters. No, after all, it isn't a curable wound or infection or allergic outburst or ideopathic lesion, as we had hoped, and for which the vet had been treating her over the past few months. It's a cancerous tumor, slowly but inexorably increasing in size. And at its current rate of growth, the thing might force us to put her down before the winter is out, before the snow has melted or the ground thawed enough to bury her on the back lot. Our other cat, Calliope, died at about the same time of the year, as did our first two dogs, Crispin and Pendragon, so we weren't able to bury any of them in the backyard.

Some things, it seems, don't ever change.

The force of that truth drove us to a riverside restaurant, where we watched the water pour sleekly over an old power dam, roil up in waves, then ripple by a snow- and ice-covered sandbar, aswarm with Canada geese and mallard ducks. A line of woods along the farther shore seemed motionless through the haze of falling snow. Near the end of lunch, the sandbar turned out to be a melting ice floe, as we discovered when it suddenly turned completely around in midriver and started floating and dissolving downstream, the geese and ducks abandoning it one by one, until it passed completely out of sight.

SATURDAY / JANUARY 7

Last night around midnight, Kate and I went for a snow walk with Pip. The streets are so quiet then — no traffic, no joggers, no barking dogs or screeching crows — that the silence is almost palpable. Especially in a newly fallen snow, which seems to muffle even the faintest sounds, so one's ears are virtually shut down and everything visible becomes much more vivid. The frozen snowflakes glittering under the light of the streetlamps. The darkened houses looming out of the white landscape. The shadows of tree trunks cutting across the snow. The snow weighing down the branches of junipers and spruces. The whole world mysteriously transformed into a study of dark and light. Quintessence of winter at night. Except for Pip, pulling hard on the leash, as if he knew exactly where he was headed, despite his beginning to develop cataracts. Terriers, even supposedly docile Welsh terriers like Pip, pay attention to nothing but the dictates of their noses. For them, the world is always a study of droppings and waterings — damnably difficult to detect under the cover of new snow.

This morning when I first looked out the kitchen window, I was so distracted by the snow that I didn't notice the dark shape huddled on the right side of the bird feeder just a few feet beyond the window. But when Kate came down and looked out, she abruptly reported "There's a bird on the feeder, and it looks like it's dead." A few minutes later, "No, it's not dead. It's moving a bit. But you'd better move it somewhere else. It's blocking the other birds from feeding." Actually, the bird was only taking up one side of the four-sided feeder tray, and I didn't feel like going out in my pajamas to move it. "Let's give it a few minutes," I said, "and see what happens." Had I noticed it was a sparrow, I'd have told her there was a special providence in it. But the thing was so hunched up I couldn't tell whether it was a finch, a junco, a pine siskin, a sparrow, or some other kind of small bird. I watched it off and on the next hour or so, and it didn't budge much, except when a starling pushed it aside momentarily. But then it hunkered down again in the same spot. I wondered whether it was suffering from the cold. Kate wondered whether it had flown into the kitchen window, as other birds have in the past, and was trying to recover its senses. Then, just as the clouds began to break up and the sun began to break through, the bird shook its head a bit and suddenly flew off with such force that it left the feeder shuddering back and forth on its pole. It was nine o'clock at that point, two hours later than the birds ordinarily waken at this time of year. But for that particular sparrow, it was not time to rise until the sun had risen.

SUNDAY / JANUARY 8

"Look at these onions! Dutch onions. Sweet yellows and mild reds. And they're both keepers." Kate was holding up one of the new spring catalogues for me to look at, when she came into the kitchen this morning. I, on the other hand, was gazing at the large brown eggs on the white kitchen counter. And the swiss cheese and the asiago I'd just finished grating. Also the parsley and scallions to be minced for the special Sunday morning omelet I was about to cook for her. But even if I hadn't been pondering an omelet to be, I wouldn't have been thinking about onions to come or anything else in the spring garden. Not even after my brief flirtation with the Shepherd's catalogue cover the other afternoon. Such a strange turnaround from years past that I found myself wondering why I was so averse to such thoughts just then. Twenty-five winters ago, after we first moved into our present home, I could barely think about anything but the spring garden. Drawing charts, reading books, I pored over the Burpee catalogue day in and day out, reading the descriptions for each vegetable and the characteristics of each different variety as if I were studying for a final exam in vegetable gardening. It was all so fresh to me then. And relatively simple, too, given that Burpee's was the only catalogue I knew about. I was beguiled by its convenient little bull's-eyes in the margin to signify the recommended varieties, the big bull's-eyes to identify Burpee's own hybrids, and the red-white-and-blue shields to signify the All-American varieties. How could I go wrong? But a year or two later, I discovered Harris' Seeds, and a year after that it was Stokes's and then Gurney's and Henry Field's and Earl May's and Nichol's Garden Nursery and Park's and Johnny's and Vermont Bean Seed and Shumway's and Cook's and Jung's and Tomato Growers and Seeds of Change. So many catalogues that our dining-room table isn't big enough to spread them all out in front of me, even if I add a leaf or two from the closet. And it's not just all the catalogues to be surveyed, but all the different varieties of each vegetable, hybrid and heritage, domestic and foreign, to be compared and then comparatively priced. No wonder I'm more interested in the covers of the catalogues than their contents and would much prefer to contemplate an omelet, even an omelet for Kate rather than for me. Actually, I tasted a bit of the omelet — she always lures me into a bite or two — just before sitting down to my heart-healthy bowl of shredded wheat, blueberries, and one-percent acidophilus milk. The omelet, I'm pleased to report, was as intense as the bright orange light of the sun on the eastern horizon. The only thing missing were some fresh spring chives from the garden.

MONDAY / JANUARY 9

The only thing missing outside is a few more inches of snow to build up the cover a bit more. But the weather forecasters are buoyantly predicting a gradual warmup this week, until temperatures reach the high thirties, possibly even the low forties by Wednesday. Not a happy prospect, since it'll gradually melt down the snowcover we've accumulated over the last week, leaving Kate's perennial bed and my row-covered vegetables exposed to the harsh temperatures and winds of January and February. Kate, as usual, is in touch with the season — "What's wrong with cold weather in January?" And I agree, but then I can't help remembering how, just a few weeks ago, both of us had thought about planting another crop of radishes, as if we were happily contemplating an abnormally long run of warm weather. We are, it seems, as fickle as the weather.

And I, it seems, am more changeable than I ever imagined — a professor of English, of literary nonfiction, of the personal essay, writing about something as impersonal as winter. No wonder I've felt a bit strange and uncomfortable the past week or so, as I've wandered around the yard and the neighborhood, observing the snow and the birds and the angle of the sun in the eastern sky and the shadows of the trees upon the snow with the seriousness of intent I'd ordinarily devote to the words and phrases of a literary text. As if I could interpret them, like a meteorologist or a seer, when I sometimes don't know the first thing about what I'm seeing or feeling, except that I've been seeing and feeling such things for sixty-three years. Maybe I should get a few books about the weather, about reading the clouds and looking for other signs of winter. Like the location of the Big Dipper, sixty degrees above the horizon in the western sky at three o'clock this morning. Or the coral and purple sunrise in the southeastern horizon between seven and seven-thirty this morning. But now that I think of it, I wonder how I'm going to keep up with winter once the new semester begins next week and I'm back to teaching my graduate essay course again.

Maybe I should stick to the things I really know about, like our first vegetarian lasagna of the new year, laced with a couple pints of basil- and garlic-flavored tomato sauce that I cooked up and froze last August from our first big harvest of the season. A sauce that Kate enriched this evening with an infusion of sliced mushrooms, sautéed in olive oil and red wine. Oh yes, there were the usual cheeses — the lowfat mozzarella, alternating with a mixture of asiago and parmesan blended with the lowfat ricotta and the drained, chopped spinach, as only Kate can blend them all together. But the memory of high summer emanating from that sauce was enough to get me thinking of the garden once again, even to the point of contemplating a session or two with all those spring catalogues.

TUESDAY / JANUARY 10

The snowcover is dwindling, the streets are slushy, and the promised warmup doesn't feel any warmer at all. The moisture in the air is almost as harsh as the windchill factors of last week. The air so dense with it this morning that I felt it cutting into my skin all the way down to the office. Thank God for the mixed-bean and pork soup that Kate cooked up yesterday for lunches the next few days — a richly textured concoction of sixteen different kinds of beans, defatted pork broth and diced pork, her homemade tomato juice, a chopped onion, an Anaheim pepper, chili powder, and the juice of a lemon. One of the best ways I know to weather a foggy winter day at the office.

Foggy as it is, the moisture here is nothing compared to the torrents of rain inundating California from north to south, from the Pacific coast inland to the Central Valley. Seventeen inches in some places during the past week, and more to come during the next few days. No wonder my son-in-law, Monty, says, "This storm actually feels as if it's coming off the ocean, wave after wave of it." But I'm momentarily nonplussed when my daughter Hannah gets on the phone and asks me, "Do you remember the hurricane that struck when we were living in Maine?" Then she reminds me of the ninety-mile-an-hour winds and "the sheets of rain," and I quickly recall the hurricane of 1960. And so does Kate, who witnessed it when she was living in upstate New York. None of us is an island entire of itself, especially when it comes to violent weather. It unites us in a community of shared experience and feeling, though we are miles apart in distance and years apart in age.

The weather in California is remarkably violent, and Hannah offers me some haunting images to document its forcefulness — a lemon tree blown over just a few feet from her house, garden greens buried in mud, worms crawling on her kitchen floor — but she sounds strangely detached in her discussion of it. And she doesn't hesitate to reflect on her own sense of calmness. "It hasn't really affected us yet in any seriously damaging way." I remember feeling similarly detached for a while during the disastrous Midwest flood of 1993, because our house is on a sloping lot, on very high ground, a mile and a half from the Iowa River that cuts through the center of town. Two months into the flood, though, water began trickling down the stone walls of our basement and seeping through the cracks in the concrete floor from the saturated clay ground around it. Then black watermarks started appearing in the ceiling of our attic study. And before it was over we had to have the chimney torn down and rebuilt, the attic walls repainted, and the second-floor bedrooms repapered. In a great flood, I discovered, there is no high ground.

WEDNESDAY / JANUARY 11

In a great fog, as I discovered this morning, there's no ground at all. No there there. Only here. A fog so dense that even looking out the attic window, I couldn't see any farther than a block away. The familiar background of trees and houses had virtually disappeared, leaving only the foreground of our immediate neighborhood. But that was enough to consume my attention, for yesterday's warmup to the mid thirties followed by last night's freezing temperatures had produced a heavy coating of rime on all the shrubs and trees. A patina of hoarfrost backed by a veil of dense fog. White on white. Winter art. A monochromatic landscape.

Even the smallest touches of color stand out. The pale raspberry breast of the redpoll pecking in the snow below the feeder. The oval red fruit of the barberry that I pass on my walk down to the office. The faded brown leaves still hanging on oak trees, especially the lower branches of the pin oaks — all the edges and deep indentations of their leaves meticulously outlined with frost. From a short distance away, the rimy edging looks like a solid white outline. Up close, it turns into a string of crystals, thousands — or possibly even millions — of them edging each leaf.

The farther I walk, the more I notice that the fog is not so thick as it had seemed, or that it's not quite as pervasive as I'd thought. Or perhaps it's thinning out even as I'm walking through it. At ground level, I can see six or seven blocks down the street — the densest fog, it seems, is well above eye level, thirty or forty feet up. The farther I walk the more I notice that the landscape is not as monochromatic as I'd thought. The frosted edging of the oak leaves is distinctly whiter than the rime coating on the spruce trees. The rime on the spruces and other evergreens covers only their east sides — there must have been a slight wind after midnight — and the coating is grayer on the spruces than on the hemlocks, which seem pale greenish white by comparison. The gray mist of the fog seems whiter than the precast concrete surfaces of the modern riverside buildings, but not as dense and therefore not as white as the exhaust coming from the smokestack of the riverside powerplant.

I'm beginning to get a faint idea of what it might be like to look at an arctic landscape through the eyes of an Eskimo.

THURSDAY / JANUARY 12

Now I wonder whether the Eskimos have as many words for gray skies or sunless days as they do for snow and ice — it's beginning to look like I could use a few myself. The sun hasn't shown its face here in Iowa City for four days, since it exited right after putting on that coral and purple light show early Monday morning. And it probably won't show up again for at least another four days, given the moist air that's now coming our way from the Pacific deluge of the past week. Did I say the sun seems to shine more brightly in January than at any other time of the year? I must have been seeing things, or thinking of some other place, like the coast of Maine or the leeward side of Kauai. But the fog has lifted, the hoarfrost has disappeared, the warming temperatures have continued to hold in the mid thirties, so the forgetfulness of last week's all-embracing snow is now just a memory.

Talk about memory! Kate sure hasn't let me forget the spring gardening catalogues. Every day, it seems, she's paging her way through one or two of them, whether she's reading in bed or watching TV. And she's not just scouring the new flower offerings for her own garden. She's also checking out the vegetables too. Today, for example, she was trying to ring my bell with a newfangled version of an old-fashioned kind of spud called "fingerling potatoes." I haven't grown potatoes for some ten years or so, given how chilly and damp our soil tends to be when it's best to plant them in early spring. But Kate sure does know how to get under the skin of my resolve—"Just imagine how good they'd taste in a French potato salad with our own fresh herbs, along with some fresh sliced cucumbers and our own tomatoes." One way of getting through winter is to think about summer.

Phoebe also knows how to work her wiles upon me. This morning for the first time in several days, she went to the back door, gave me one of her owly stares, whined to be let out, and promptly went on some of her old rounds. A stop at the Plexiglas door over the cellarway entry. A few drinks from the unfrozen part of the water-lily pond. A visit to the gazebo. Is it just the warmer weather that draws her outside? Or is it possibly the case that she's getting stronger rather than weaker, plumper rather than thinner—that the herbal remedy Kate's been giving her this week has begun to take effect?

According to our neighbor Linda, who told Kate about the stuff, "It's really strong stuff. The first few doses I took of it, I was really flying." And according to an article in an herb magazine, it's reportedly prevented recurrences and produced remissions of cancer. So Kate's now taking it to prevent a recurrence of breast cancer, as well as giving it to Phoebe. And if the stuff really works, I might try it to prevent another heart attack. Who knows what powers might lurk in a century-old concoction, created by a Canadian Ojibway medicine man, of burdock root, sheep sorrel, Turkish rhubarb root, cress, spices, and slippery elm. It certainly produces one of the slipperiest fluids I've ever seen. And for the moment, at least, it gives us the illusion of controlling something almost as slippery and uncontrollable as the weather.

FRIDAY / JANUARY 13

Skies still overcast this morning. Temperature still in the low thirties. Phoebe asking to go out again — to the cellarway, the pond, and the gazebo. A refutation at last of Heraclites' observation that you can't step into the same river twice. I had stepped into the same day twice.

But when I went to prepare my standard breakfast of shredded wheat and fruit, I suddenly realized that I'd forgotten to buy bananas on the way home yesterday, and I didn't have any frozen blueberries on hand either. A different day, after all. And a gentle reminder, I said to myself, that today is Friday the thirteenth, a day to be especially cautious and attentive. A hard task for an absent-minded professor. I was already so disconcerted by the missing bananas and blueberries that I forgot to take my daily vitamins, though I didn't realize it until just now when I started writing this report.

But I did notice some other things the minute I left home for the office. The goldfish swimming at the surface of the fully thawed lily pond. The covered spinach row sticking up through the melted snow — a reminder that I still hadn't gotten around to ordering the spring seeds for my vegetable garden. The air just a bit warmer and a bit gentler. The cloud cover a bit higher. The snowcover a bit lower. Not quite the same day as yesterday. The mere thought of those differences sharpened my attention so much that I soon found myself noticing things on campus that I hadn't seen for days or even weeks. Orange hawthorn berries covering the ground by the side of the Physics Building. Patches of grass still intensely green from the warm fall and the protective snowcover. And then, as I looked above the Physics Building, a small circular patch of white in the southeastern sky, glowing faintly through the high cloud cover.

The sun was out, after all, for anyone interested in seeing it. I kept checking on it every few seconds as I crossed the street on my way to the Prairie Lights bookstore to look for some guides to the weather. Once inside, I was eager to report my news and get back outside again, for fear it might disappear without my seeing it again. No one in the store could believe my exuberant announcement. In fact, my friends behind the counter, Jan and Jim and Paul, looked at me as if I'd lost my bearings. But when I stepped outside, it was still up there, still glowing faintly behind a scrim of clouds. By noontime, though, it was gone for the rest of the day. If the sun is shining and no one is there to see it, does it produce any light?

❧ ❧

SATURDAY / JANUARY 14

"Look to the weathers to come and the weathers that have been." Thus spake the sibylline lady Kate when I sought her oracular wisdom early this morning about the continuing gloom of the unremittingly overcast sky. So, I consulted the *Organic Gardening 1995 Almanac*, only to discover that the first week of January in Iowa had been "cloudy" rather than sunny, that the week just past had brought "snow" rather than melting snow, and that the week to come promises to be "very cold." Looking further into the future, toward the first month of spring gardening, I was transfixed by the prospect of "cold" and "snow" the last week of March, "very cold" temperatures the first week of April, “snow” in mid-April, and “sleet” at the end of April. No mention of sun in any of the predictions. Thus spake the weather almanac.

The chief meteorologist for the National Weather Service in Iowa spoke somewhat differently in yesterday’s morning newspaper. “We’re very, very frustrated,” he said, when asked about the persistent fog. And hundreds of grounded travelers throughout Iowa, evidently spoke words of similar import, not fit for reporting in a public newspaper. The state climatologist, after consulting his weather almanac, spoke of El Niño.

Faced with such gloomy and dire pronouncements, I turned for solace to the gardening catalogues, where never is heard a discouraging word and the skies are not cloudy all day. And there I found the weather I had been looking for in a colored illustration on the cover of the Vermont Bean Seed catalogue. A watercolor landscape, showing a young lad in the foreground harvesting cabbages, beans, tomatoes, beets, carrots, onions, lettuce, spinach, peppers, and pumpkins, all at once, from a roadside garden bed, leading to a gentle blue river in the middle distance, backed by a rising green hillside with bright white houses and a white church scattered along a meandering road, topped by a blue sky with a few scattered clouds, and a single monarch butterfly in midair.

That single picture spoke a thousand words to me. But the words escaped me when I absentmindedly turned my head from the catalogue on my desk and looked out the attic window at the scene in our backyard — the ice- and snow-covered stone steps in the foreground leading to the pockmarked snowfield with the empty bird feeder swinging in the middle distance, the dried stubble of the flower border near the back, the four stolid spruce trees behind, topped by an overcast sky with a single black crow in midair.

❧ ❧

SUNDAY / JANUARY 15

The glorious winters of my youth! Whatever became of them? And the snows! Where are the snows of yesteryear — the flakes falling regularly from November through March, the drifts building up above one's head, the sidewalks like trenches walled by the piled-up snow, and the lawns like virtual communities of snow forts and snowmen? Am I imagining those snows? Or did they actually take place back then — as they still seem to do — in Cleveland and other cities on Lake Erie. And if that's the case, is my love of winter just a nostalgic yearning for childhood. But then I also remember the massive snows of Ithaca, New York, during my days in graduate school at Cornell, where I once nearly lost my way — and my life — walking home in a blizzard. And I remember too the snow forts I built for my daughter Hannah in Brunswick, Maine. So perhaps the scarcity of snow over the past several winters is just the way things are here in Iowa. But Kate tells me about the big snows and the long-lasting winters of her childhood in Lisbon, Iowa, and how the plows piled it up so high along the main street that it reached almost to the top of the lampposts — "The lampposts, of course, were shorter then."

This winter we've had only two good periods of snow, one in early December that melted off before Christmas, and another in early January that's now dwindled down to just a few inches. So, in search of some more snowy weather, I went with Kate and her mother Lib to see the new movie version of *Little Women* for the second time in a week.

And I wasn't disappointed. The snow scenes in the first part of the movie were just as lush and evocative as I'd remembered them from the week before. The white stuff covering the fields as far as one could see into the distance, as the title and credits scrolled in front of it. The snow drifting along the paths and lanes of the village, then falling faintly in front of the first shot of the March family house. Oh yes, I noticed this time around that each twig of every branch, each needle on every bush was carefully flaked with snow. And I noticed too that the later snow shots of the March house were identical to the earlier ones. But it mattered not, because the snow seemed so genuine a part of everyone's life as to suggest a deep sense of connection between the quality of human existence and the season of winter. In fact, the weather throughout the movie seemed so much in the foreground as to suggest an intimate connection between the rhythm of life and the seasons of the year. Perhaps it was a yearning for that older sense of connectedness that brought tears to my eyes both last week and this. But then again, perhaps I'm just a sucker for a good old-fashioned snowstorm. Whatever the case, the weather in this movie clearly deserves an Oscar.

MONDAY / JANUARY 16

So many sunless days that people were muttering about it at the bank this morning. The fellow standing next to me at the teller's window: "It's getting pretty depressing." His teller: "I agree, but it could be worse. Just look at California." Misery loves company — especially if their misery is worse. Actually, it's far from miserable here, given temperatures in the mid thirties. And tomorrow's supposed to be even warmer, possibly in the forties, possibly along with some rain. Unusual weather for January, and the state climatologist blames it all on El Niño. So, I decided to consult my new weather books about this fabled phenomenon and discovered a fascinating story.

Though El Niño first made its way into the headlines in the early 1980s, during cataclysmic weather disturbances throughout the southern hemisphere — monsoons, floods, droughts, and forest fires — it's been known to meteorologists and Peruvian fishermen for almost a hundred years. The fishermen first noticed it in 1891, when the faltering westward trade winds that characterize El Niño allowed unusually warm surface water to move east across the Pacific and block the welling up of cold water along the Peruvian shore that ordinarily yields an abundance of anchovies. The shortage of anchovies not only impoverished the Peruvian fisherman but also resulted in a massive die-off of fish and birds that feed on anchovies. The abnormally warm counter-trade winds also brought monsoon rains, producing floods and mudslides throughout the western coast of South America. El Niños subsequently occurred in 1911, 1925, 1941, 1953, and 1957, by which time meteorologists had begun studying the relationship between wind and air pressure patterns in the Pacific Ocean and the Indian Ocean, which led to the discovery that El Niños in Peru occur at the same time as outbreaks of drought in countries ordinarily dependent on monsoons from the Indian Ocean. And now we know these interconnected aberrations have produced cataclysms throughout the world, including the Midwest flood of 1993.

All this adversity comes under the Spanish name for the Christ child — El Niño — because the phenomenon usually begins around Christmas, so the Peruvian fisherman gave it that name, either prayerfully or sarcastically. Whatever the case, it's a long way from Peruvian anchovies to overcast Iowa skies, but like many things in this world, they're connected by El Niño.

TUESDAY / JANUARY 17

Just when I was beginning to understand it, El Niño is already disappearing from the scene. Or so it would seem. How else to account for the full moon I saw out the west window this morning around six? And the reddish orange glow of Mars above it? At least, I thought it boded well for clear skies and the possibility of our first visible sunrise in eight days. So I ran upstairs to the attic to get a good view out the east windows, and there, sure enough, was a thin strip of pale blue sky between darker, horizontal banks of clouds. With that good omen in sight, I hustled back down to the second floor, to shower and shave before the coming sunrise. By the time I got dressed, though, the clear skies were gone, and so was the possibility of a visible sunrise.

But Pip rose this morning more animated than he had been yesterday at breakfast time, when he refused the three regulation milkbones he expects to find waiting for him on the edge of the breakfast table every morning after his early constitutional. This morning, as is customary, he plucked each one crisply off the table and carried it into the living room between his teeth, devouring each one separately before coming back for the next. And Phoebe jumped smartly up to the counter in the half bath, where her food bowls are located, and eagerly lapped up her Ojibway tea mix.

By that point in the morning, I felt more like a contented nanny looking over her charges than a professor getting ready for his first class of the semester. In fact, ever since I started this winter watch, I've felt somewhat like a fretful nanny, fussing over the comings and goings of the sun and the moon and the wind and the clouds and the snow and the stars, as if they were newly sprouted seedlings, when the truth, of course, is that their behavior is utterly beyond my control—and often beyond my ken. This morning, for example, on my walk down to campus, just when I was fretting about things still being out of kilter, the gray clouds began to pull away, revealing blue patches of sky and an intensely bright sun—good omens for the first day of school. And then, as if to give me another lesson in uncertainty, the sun disappeared during my midmorning class, just when I was talking very assuredly about varieties of form in the personal essay. But the disappearance of the sun at least reminded me to offer a few cautionary remarks about categorizing the form of something so personal as an essay. And then as if to underline its point, the sun returned in early afternoon and stayed long enough to produce a reddish orange sunset across the whole width of the western sky.

WEDNESDAY / JANUARY 18

The sky was so clear last night and the moon so bright I could easily see the dark-shaded craters on its surface when I went out to the compost pile. The air had finally dried out, and the wind died down, leaving a comfortable chill in the high twenties — a perfect winter night for a walk with Pip. But my thoughts were heavily overcast by reports of the catastrophic earthquake in Japan. Almost two thousand dead, more than six thousand injured, and the city of Kobe, a city of almost one and one-half million, burning out of control. In the face of such colossal suffering and loss, my winter watch seemed unspeakably trivial and beside the point. And I suddenly felt even more stung by the recollection of Kate's remarks at dinner — "You can't just go on twittering about the sun and the moon. You have to make something more of it."

I instinctively wanted to defend myself, to say that I'm not just twittering — that in writing about the sun and the moon and the clouds and the snow and the spinach, I'm really paying reverence to the things in this world that matter most deeply to me. But the words didn't come readily to my lips, especially when I was savoring the crab-stuffed flounder, steamed artichoke, and chilled sauvignon blanc we were having for dinner. And it wasn't any better this morning, not even during the rare spectacle of watching the sun rise in the east just after I'd seen the full moon set in the west, for I knew that when I went downstairs to get the morning newspaper, the front page would be covered with stories of Kobe. The front page, in fact, offered me a distinctly different kind of sunrise from the one I'd just seen — a full-width color picture, dominated by the reddish orange sweep of fire raging through the city of Kobe. And above the picture, the haunting remark of Minoru Takasu, a survivor of the quake, just a couple of years older than me — "I thought it was the end of the world."

Again my winter project seemed trivial. But then it occurred to me that I make these reports because, like Minoru Takasu, I cherish the world. I do not want to see the end of it any more than he does. I want it to continue, sunrise and sunset, moonrise and moonset, winter after winter after winter, world without end. And I want to take note of its continuance, if for no other reason than to make a record of my reverence for it. Pious sentiments, I realize. But those are the only pieties I know.

THURSDAY / JANUARY 19

Finally more snow — three inches of it this morning. So, the weather at last seems to be getting back to normal, or at least something akin to what one might expect in January. (Given the way winters have been going around here lately, I'm beginning to think that a normal winter exists only in the meteorologists' numerical averages.) Things are also settling down in California, where the rain has stopped falling, at least for the time being. But it'll be a while before things even begin to settle down in Kobe and the other quake-ridden cities of Japan. More than three thousand dead, fifteen thousand injured, twenty thousand buildings damaged or destroyed, and the cost of rebuilding projected to run between twenty and sixty billion. Such a prodigious catastrophe that I could hardly keep my mind on the quaint essay by Margaret Mead that we were talking about in class this morning—"A Day in Samoa." Talk about cognitive dissonance! In one part of my mind I was tracking the daily routines of that remote South Seas village, and in the other part I was ruminating on death and devastation in a vast urban complex, wondering what I (or Margaret Mead) might write about a day in Kobe. The repair bill is quickly catching more attention than anything else, as I learned from an article in the *New York Times*—"Through Kobe's Rubble, An Economic Rainbow." So, it seems, the languishing economy of Japan will be given a big boost by the quake.

I first discovered that bad weather is big business during the flood of '93. A colleague in philosophy assured me one day during a driving rainstorm that the agricultural losses would easily be offset by the economic stimulus of rebuilding or repairing all the damaged roads, bridges, homes, and other structures. "It'll probably turn out to be a wash, if not better." And sure enough, the state of Iowa is now running a surplus, whereas two years ago its books were still in the red. The zero-sum game of calamity. Good weather, on the other hand, doesn't seem anywhere near so profitable. Last summer, the nearly ideal alternation of sun and rain, together with moderate temperatures in the mid to upper eighties, produced such a bumper crop that corn prices plummeted in the face of the surplus grain piled up outside elevators around the state.

By this logic, we should all be gearing up for the most profitable weather event of all — the predicted collision a few hundred million years from now of the Cartwheel Galaxy and the Milky Way. Imagine the stimulus to come from intergalactic rebuilding, and how it will boost the economy of the universe. For the time being, though, I'm just savoring the new snow piling up outside, reinsulating the row-covered spinach, boosting the chances that my two covered artichoke plants might actually make it through the winter.

FRIDAY / JANUARY 20

The north wind — a speciality of winter. I first sensed its doings today around two in the morning, when I looked out the west window of our bedroom and saw that the heavy overcast of yesterday's snowstorm had been blown away, leaving a much higher ceiling of scattered clouds. Then around quarter to six, when I was up again, I looked out the window and saw that the clouds had almost passed over, leaving a clear sky, the waning moon above the spruce trees, and a few wisps rapidly moving south. Then around seven-thirty, when I let Pip and Phoebe out, I saw that the sky had clouded over again, and felt a harsh gust moving at around twenty-five miles an hour.

Some wind. Enough to turn a temperature reading of twenty-five above into a windchill of seven below. Enough to bring me back inside just seconds after I had picked the morning newspaper off the front porch. Enough to turn my attention from the newly fallen snow I'd been yearning for just a few days ago to the gales that had been driving it our way all yesterday morning and early afternoon.

A blowhard. It screeched and whined through the attic windows, taking me back some forty years to the time I first heard about the windharp — the harp of Aeolus, god of the winds — and built one out of balsa wood. A long rectangular instrument that I fitted out with a sound hole and four violin strings tuned in unison, then placed atilt in pull-down windows to hear "nature's breath," as the Romantic poets were wont to call it.

But hardly inspiring. Especially when it cut at my face on the way to the office this morning. It seemed calm when Kate and I first left the house, probably because we were walking south, with our backs to it. But when we turned west, it was suddenly there, and I remarked that it must be coming from that direction. Kate, as usual, was not misled about the direction of things: "It's not coming from the west, it's coming from the north." And just a few seconds later we encountered a small stake in the ground, holding two pink ribbons suspended in midair toward the south.

The north wind. Its edge was so sharp I kept my face down almost all the way down to the office. But just before turning into the building I sensed a momentary aura of light around me and looked up to see the sun, shining white behind a veil of swirling clouds, each one casting it in a different shade of white.

The wind. From the Sanskrit *vati*, meaning "it blows."

❧ ❧

SATURDAY / JANUARY 21

One month beyond the winter solstice, and we're deep into the kind of weather that sends farmers, retirees, and other "snowbirds" south to places like the Texas and Florida gulf coasts. The kind of weather that gives a special punch to TV ads touting cold remedies, snow tires, ski lessons, rock salt, and Caribbean love boats. The kind of weather that tells me to pull on my heavy wool socks, long johns, t-shirt, flannel shirt, and sweatshirt, and enjoy the simple pleasure of keeping warm on a bitterly cold day. The temperature this morning just ten above and the north wind gusting up to thirty-five miles an hour for a windchill factor of twenty below. Not exactly the sort of weather to tempt even the cross-country skiers outside.

But shortly before noon this morning, when I was up in the attic scanning the landscape, touching up some of my previous reports, and thinking about the one for today, I noticed Kate lugging our large split-oak harvesting basket back and forth between the house and the gazebo. She'd mentioned something the other day about having to defrost the basement freezer, but not wanting to do so until the weather turned cold enough so she could temporarily store the frozen produce outside. But I'd forgotten the plan, so when I ran downstairs to ask her what she was doing, her answer momentarily brought me up short.

"I'm just making something of winter."

And so she was. At the north end of the gazebo, she'd carefully piled up all the frozen cartons, containing all the beef broth and duck broth she'd made during the fall, the fresh gulf shrimp we'd bought this summer and fall, and all the tomato purée and spaghetti sauce we'd made from the bumper harvest of tomatoes this summer. At the south end of the gazebo, she'd set up a large cardboard carton filled with ducks from a local farmer's wife, chicken pot pies she'd made a few weeks ago, and ice cube trays of frozen pesto that I'd made from the bumper crop of basil this summer and fall. The box was closed, the top weighted down with a heavy stone garden turtle to protect the stuff inside from the neighbor's untethered dog.

But the mere sight of it all having come back outside to the gazebo at the edge of the garden on one of the coldest days of the winter gave me a sudden feeling of intense warmth, a renewed sense of the deep interconnectedness of things in the rhythm of the seasons, and a new understanding of Shelley's timely question: "If winter comes can spring be far behind?"

"You bet," said Kate, the point of which I could feel acutely in every one of my chilled fingertips after carrying all the frozen boxes back in again.

❧ ❧

SUNDAY / JANUARY 22

Snow flurries this morning — the first of the season. Swirling in from the northwest. Also swirling up from the ground in gusts and eddies, a visible reminder that the wind is variable. Driving in a strong general direction, but also taking sudden detours along the way. Pushed in one direction or another by the contours of a building, the slope of a landscape, or the run of a windbreak. The invisible wind made visible in the flurried movements of the snow.

The flurries are so light and the ground gusts so strong that the sidewalks and streets seem as if they're continuously being dusted and swept clean. The backyard snowscape has also been swept by the wind, rippling and ruffling in some spots, arrestingly smooth in others. Bird tracks, rabbit tracks, squirrel tracks, and deer tracks completely erased overnight. And Kate's tracks to the bird feeder gradually turning into shallow scallops, merging into the smooth contours of the surrounding snow.

The atmosphere is so cold and dry that the flakes glisten in the air and glitter on the snow. Especially in midmorning, when Kate and I are having brunch in the kitchen, and the sun is gradually beginning to break through. The flakes look like minuscule bits of diamond or flecks of gold. Kate says, "They look like pyrite. Fool's gold." And they do, especially when their glitter suddenly disappears. So magical, it's momentarily hard to keep my attention on the fresh onion bagels, the smoked lemon-pepper trout, the goat cheese, sliced tomatoes, capers, onions, lettuce, and garlic-stuffed olives. A flurry of food that finally rivals the flakes outside.

By late afternoon, the snow flurries have ended, the blue hour descended, and the wind died down. And now, a few hours before midnight, the wind is picking up again, and low-level clouds are again coming out of the northwest, as if the day will end much as it began — like an emblem of the year, the cycle of the seasons, each one leading gradually but inexorably into the next and inexorably back to itself. Another reminder that winter passeth, spring cometh, and I still haven't started making my seed orders.

❧ ❧

MONDAY / JANUARY 23

According to my calendar, the gardening season begins on the day I sit down at the dining-room table with my favorite catalogues, the records of my seed orders from the last few years, the January seed-review issues of my favorite gardening magazines, the plastic box from the refrigerator containing all the seed packets I've carried over from recent years, the *Organic Gardening Encyclopedia* entry listing the years of viability for each kind of vegetable seed — and begin planning our two vegetable gardens. No wonder I put it off until today. Last year I didn't start working on it until late February.

Kate, of course, has already made her way through all the catalogues, and for all I know is rereading them just to make sure she hasn't overlooked any other old-fashioned or newfangled vegetables to push my way. Hutterite beans and Japanese greens. I, as usual, have dutifully nodded my interest each time. But in truth, I've only glanced at a few catalogues in passing, just to see what's going on in the world of peppers and tomatoes. It's not that I'm reluctant to do my part. It's just that the task seems to get more complicated each year, and not just because the seed companies have become more numerous and their offerings more various, but because I've evidently become more compulsive in my methods of selection.

This morning, for example, I spent half an hour weighing the relative merits of eight different pickling cucumbers, which involved me in consulting ten gardening catalogues, before I finally settled on three choices that I was leaning toward even before I started (Cross Country, Homemade, and Liberty). Forty years ago, when I first took up vegetable gardening, I just went to the local hardware store in April and bought a few tomato plants, pepper plants, and several packets of seed right off the racks. Now, it often takes me three or four days to get through all that stuff on the dining-room table.

But today, surprisingly, I was able to get through most of my selections by early afternoon, before going down to the office for a few hours. If I didn't know any better, I'd have said it went so quickly because most of last year's choices turned out to be so tasty and productive, and most of this year's varieties come with less than rave reviews. But I'm not done yet, and Kate never orders her flower seeds until I'm finished, so it could be February again before we're fully underway. And what if it takes that long? What's the hurry? Winter's still with us, and I'm all for taking my seasons one at a time. Winter now. Spring later.

TUESDAY / JANUARY 24

"A few simple pleasures," as Kate calls them — a Mineola tangelo, a freshly ground cup of Kona coffee, a few squares of Swiss bittersweet chocolate — and I was up often enough after midnight to watch the moon gradually make its way from east to west across the southern sky. It was still clearly visible at eight-thirty this morning when I started walking down to the office to teach my nine-thirty class, and it seemed much more invigorated than I. Probably because it appeared to be moving higher and higher as it moved westward in the pale blue sky. Also because it didn't have any wine with dinner.

The entire sky was so clear late last night that when I put Pip out for a brief airing, I quickly noticed the Big Dipper on the north side, its cup inverted over our neighbor's house. I couldn't help wondering at that moment what stars might be visible to the three hundred thousand homeless people of Kobe, and discovered upon checking our stellarscope that anyone over there, looking up in the same direction as I, would have seen the constellation Phoenix. I hope someone was paying attention just then. The Japanese stock market evidently doesn't pay attention to the stars, given today's report in the *New York Times* that "it suffered severe aftershocks from last week's earthquake." I'm more troubled, though, by the aftershocks of Shizuko Hirajima, who suddenly lost most of her hearing after listening to the screams of her dying neighbors. Who in such circumstances would want to be fitted with a pair of hearing aids?

When I got my first pair of aids several years ago, the first sound I remember hearing that bright spring day was the rush of wind by my ears. I'd evidently been out of touch with it for so long that I'd completely forgotten what it sounded like. And then the clatter of leaves in the wind. And then birdsong. And then the realization that in losing some of my upper-register hearing, I'd been missing the drift not just of cocktail chatter or of soft-spoken students, but also of the weather. A light rain beginning to fall, the distant rumble of a storm beginning to blow in, the hush of a late night snow. Who in such circumstances would not want to be fitted with a pair of hearing aids?

There are times, of course, when I too wish it were possible to tune out some of the weather in my life. The all-night thunderstorms, the all-day windstorms, the summer hailstorms, and the crackling sounds of a winter ice storm. Yet even such noise is music to my ears when I contemplate Mrs. Hirajima's deafness.

WEDNESDAY / JANUARY 25

Another strikingly clear sky last night when I went out with Pip, the Big Dipper again inverted over my neighbor's house. And the waning moon visible again in the southern sky when I got up around seven, along with a few alternating strands of reddish orange light and bluish gray clouds in the southeastern horizon. A few more predictably clear nights, clear days, and temperatures in the twenties to low thirties, and I just might go into the weather-forecasting business myself. Chuck these daily winter reports and become a long-ranger. Make my own almanac.

The National Weather Service, it seems, is now going into long-range forecasting with a vengeance. Instead of limiting themselves to one- and three-month forecasts, indicating "the chances" that a particular area might be warmer or colder, wetter or drier, than usual, the folks at the weather service have just started issuing six-month and yearlong predictions, with a reportedly higher degree of probability than before. Thanks, it turns out, to El Niño, which has been occurring so frequently during the past several years that its presence or absence can now be factored in to produce more reliable long-range forecasts. Catastrophe is the mother of invention.

Just imagine what one might do with such reliable predictions. Sell options on the regions that have been heavily targeted for wetter than normal conditions — the entire Sunbelt this February, March, and April — on the assumption that heavy flooding will lead to massive government assistance and economic rebuilding programs, as in the Midwest two years ago and California this year. Or somewhat closer to home, I might buy derivatives to insure myself against the drier than normal conditions that are likely to afflict Iowa gardeners this spring.

Or am I just reinventing the wheel? The futures market? The Chicago Board of Trade? But with a much lower level of risk.

Come to think of it, that's the only thing that bothers me about all this long-range forecasting — that the gain in probability might lead to a loss of uncertainty and all the pleasure that comes therefrom. Now, as things stand, those weather projections are so new and untested that I don't yet have any idea of whether things will pan out exactly as the weather service predicts. So, I can still worry incessantly — and pester Kate — about when to plant, how deeply to plant, how much to water, and God knows what else. Uncertainty, after all, is such a fruitful state of mind that nothing should be done to thwart it.

THURSDAY / JANUARY 26

When I saw the Big Dipper again last night, and the crescent moon in the northern sky, I began to feel as if the clear skies of the past few days might actually hang on for several more days, possibly a week. Or even longer. There's something about a run of weather — cold or hot, wet or dry, clear or cloudy, windy or calm — that seems to be endowed with an air of inevitability. And immutability. And to some extent, of course, weather does feed upon itself. A heavy snowcover helps to retain or intensify a cold front. The flood of 1993 left so much moisture on the ground, in the rivers, and in the air that the rains perpetuated themselves.

But the floods did end, and so will this run of clear, mild, sunny, and almost windless days, as I've learned from my new weather books — and from personal experience. So, I was particularly alert this morning, not wanting to miss anything that might soon be overcast or blown away by the wind. The pale mauve clouds along the northwest horizon, edged with a hint of yellowish light shortly before sunrise. The pale blue tint of the sky just then. The pale coral radiance along the southeast horizon. The long dark shadows of the walnuts slanting sharply toward the house at sunrise, the snow between them tinted faintly orange and speckled with the glitter of frozen flakes. The faint coating of hoarfrost on the spruces and yews. Everything so pale and evanescent.

But my shadow stayed with me all the way down to the office, walking just a bit to the right of me, with a much bigger and surer step than mine. Probably because it wasn't feeling any of the lower back pain I was experiencing just then. Also because it wasn't remembering how I'd gotten that pain some forty years ago, trying to lift a snow-covered lid off a well, single-handedly. Also because it wasn't noticing how that pain now returns almost every year at this time, as if I were bound to an annual season of penance. The follies of youth are visited upon the aged — especially in winter.

Just when I was congratulating myself for that chilly bit of wisdom, I looked up and noticed Kate's young cousin Stuart, a grad student here, walking jauntily toward me, his hair wet, his cheeks flush, his jacket unbuttoned, his shirt collar open. And it was almost more than memory could bear to see myself reborn again, ready to do anything in any kind of weather. We talked briefly about our computers, but nothing he said sticks so clearly in my mind as the wave of his hand and the bounce in his step as I turned to finish walking to class for a discussion of Hoagland's "A Run of Bad Luck."

❧ ❧

FRIDAY / JANUARY 27

Talk about bad luck! This morning it was freezing rain — another speciality of winter. Seemingly far from "the possibility of snow" that the weather services had been predicting over the last two days. But closer than one might suppose, as I discovered from my weather books. All it takes is an intermediate layer of warm air to melt the snow on the way down and low-level air chilly enough to freeze the intensely cool rain on impact. And once it starts falling and freezing, the terrain's as unstable as the air above it.

This morning at eight the sky was still dark gray, but nothing yet coming down. By eight-thirty, the rain was falling and patches of steely blue ice rapidly forming over depressions in the backyard snow. A menacing spectacle to anyone contemplating a mile and a half distance between home and office. Not a day for walking, but not much better for driving. By nine-fifteen, the windows of the car were covered with a layer so thick I needed a spray can of windshield de-icer to melt it. And slipping down the driveway, I wondered if I'd ever get back up again. But by nine-thirty, the street ice had already turned to slush under the pressure of traffic. The parking lot, though, was still iced over. Everyone moving mincingly. Little steps, little steps. By eleven o'clock, the ground air had already warmed up enough to prevent the rain from freezing on impact. But the water on top of ice on top of snow had produced a slick and slippery layering of stuff, treacherous enough to provoke a rare cancellation of classes — only the second or third in the history of the university. Also a call from Kate advising me to "pack all the stuff you need for the weekend and get home while you can still get back and get up the driveway." But by noon, the rain had temporarily stopped, and the drive home was as trouble-free as the one down — the roads still slushy and easily negotiable, the layer of snow on our steep driveway still free enough of ice to provide a purchase for the wheels.

At twelve-thirty, the rain started falling again, just when I was sitting down to a bowl of Kate's split pea soup, dense not only with the garlic-, bay-, thyme- and cayenne-flavored purée of peas, but also with diced onions, carrots, celery, potatoes, and low-fat ham. So perfect a counterpoint to the weather that I couldn't help feeling a special affection for a storm that could enrich so rich a concoction. By the time I was finishing my second bowl of soup, the newly fallen rain had visibly thickened the glistening sheath of ice on the tree branches, lengthened the icicles a bit along the edges of the eaves troughs, and polished up the coating on the stone steps leading to the back porch. Even without any appreciable wind, the cowbirds and sparrows slid backward a bit on the ice-covered snow whenever they bent over to peck at the seeds. Another brief rainfall, two hours later, thickened the coatings and lengthened the icicles just a bit more. So, after dinner, when the temperature has dropped once again and the water refrozen, the entire landscape should be a glisteningly hazardous ice field. Just right for savoring tomorrow's bowl of pea soup.

SATURDAY / JANUARY 28

Up this morning at six-thirty and immediately I'm surprised by a newly fallen snow, flaked on the spruces and yews (and yesterday's ice) almost as neatly as in the movie of *Little Women*. But I'm not up this early to admire the snow. I'm up to take part in Iowa's "1995 Winter Bird Feeder Survey."

Not a single bird shows up between six-thirty and seven, and only one sparrow for a fleeting stop between seven and seven-fifteen. I wonder whether anyone sent a notice of the survey to the birds themselves. Then, just as the sky begins to lighten up, the light begins to dawn in me as well — the snow has covered up all the seed. None of it visible on the ground or in the feeder trays. The weather has interfered with the survey. So I pull on my boots, run out in my pajamas, scrape the snow out of the feeders, scatter new seed beneath them, and run back in to start counting. Immediately I'm rewarded with a handful of sparrows. But I can't tell them apart. Can't tell a white-crowned sparrow from a white-throated sparrow from a tree sparrow, a house sparrow, a song sparrow, or Harris' sparrow, all of which are listed on the survey sheet. The sparrows are as confusing as the "Confusing Fall Warblers" in Peterson's *Field Guide to the Birds*. And they won't sit still long enough for me to match them up with the pictures in the book. Gradually I catch on, and by eight-thirty I can tell a house sparrow from a white-crowned sparrow from a tree sparrow. But I can't learn all the sparrows at the same time that I'm trying to count the starlings sixty feet away and make sure they're not cowbirds. And I've only seen a few colorful birds — one cardinal, one blue jay, one black-capped chickadee. No woodpeckers, no finches, no nuthatches. What are the survey people going to think of us when they look at our tally? What is Kate going to say when she comes down and discovers that I've seen so many gang birds and so few standouts. Then, as if the wish were father to the birds, a redpoll and purple finch suddenly appear. Then Kate appears, looks at the tally, looks out the window, and sure enough starts asking the embarrassing questions: "No woodpeckers? Only one cardinal?" Why do I take it so personally? It's only a survey, after all. Then she spots a mourning dove; I, a second cardinal. And before you know it, we're momentarily carried away at the prospect of topping each of our counts. But increasingly we find ourselves absorbed by the growing number of cowbirds. Forty at one sighting. And haunted by the disappointingly small number of standout birds. One flicker and no other woodpeckers. Tomorrow's another day of the survey. But for now, I just wish I'd stuck with the weather. It was a real standout. Especially after the declining sun broke through and lit up the sky, the snow, and the glistening branches of the ice-covered trees.

SUNDAY / JANUARY 29

A windless evening and a starry sky presaged an intensely bright sunrise. But at seven-fifteen this morning I was still so preoccupied with the second day of the winter bird survey that I was momentarily surprised by the light radiating once again from all the ice-covered twigs and branches of the apple, maple, and walnut trees. And the lilac bushes along the lot line. And even the dried chrysanthemums at the edge of the gazebo. Glitter everywhere. On the freeze-crusted surface of the snowscape, the ice-crusted needles of the yew bush, and the snow-covered branches of the juniper. Glitzy accents in the sky, too —

jet trails angling southeast across the path of the rising sun. So many special effects I almost forgot about my birdwatching duties.

Once again, the birds were late for breakfast. But today I was ready for them when they started coming. I'd learned a few more sparrows, so I was able to detect the arrival of three white-throated males. And our tallies from yesterday were already so high for the gang birds — the starlings, house sparrows, and cowbirds — that I didn't have to worry much about counting to arrive at "the highest number seen for each species." I was free just to watch the table manners of the birds.

The black-capped chickadee darts in to the feeder, pecks a seed off the tray, and darts off to a nearby branch to crack it and savor it. The female cardinal flies in and settles down at the feeder for a few minutes, pecking up sunflower seeds, working her beak back and forth to shell and cast out their black hulls, while the male waits his turn on the ground below or on a branch overhead, chasing off any competing male who invades his territory. The juncos stay on the ground and keep to themselves, pecking up whatever falls from the feeder overhead. The sparrows hang out in bunches in the lilac bush a few feet away, waiting for moments when the feeder is vacant or the ground below is open, but the group scatters as soon as a larger bird appears.

The cowbirds, however, are not bothered by anyone else. They move in, take over the feeder, trash the tray, scatter the seeds, hog the perches, peck at each other, push their youngsters away, and beak away any other birds that try to land at the feeder. They behave like the Serbs in Croatia, the Russians in Chechnya, the Nazis in Europe, the Turks in Armenia, Cortez in Mexico, Columbus in the West Indies. Suddenly, I find myself unable to watch them any longer. So I head off to the supermarket to pick up a few things for our Sunday brunch, but the spectacle of people shoving and pushing their carts around, myself included, makes me think of those damned cowbirds again, when I'd much rather be pondering the snow and the ice. The birds can fend for themselves.

MONDAY / JANUARY 30

So now I'm back to surveying the skies. The only problem is that they're as unmanageable as the birds. The local weather reports last night predicted clear skies and sunny weather for today. But the sky was overcast at midnight and again this morning. What's going on here? Clouds get stalled? Upper-level winds becalmed? Or another front moving in? Time to check the Internet. So I pulled up the National Weather Service reports for Iowa and discovered from a forecast filed at four-fifteen this morning that we were supposed to be having "flurries" and "gradual clearing." But then "increasing cloudiness late." That doesn't leave much room for clearing. And whatever happened to the "flurries"? If the folks at the weather service can't predict the weather just a few hours in advance, how are they going to manage it six or twelve months in advance — even with the help of El Niño?

But why should I expect so much of them, when I can't produce an accurate reading of things closer to home? Ever since we started giving Phoebe that Ojibway tea mix a few weeks ago, I've been keeping a closer eye on her than usual. Every evening, in fact, when I mix up some of the brew that Kate's prepared with a little milk and sugar, and carry Phoebe down to her bowl, I try to feel whether she's heavier or lighter, whether her coat's shinier or duller, whether she's more or less alert, whether the lesion on her hindquarters is growing or shrinking. For the first week or so of the treatment, it seemed as if all the signs were good — better appetite, slightly heavier weight, shinier coat, more alertness, more vigor, and an apparently shrinking lesion. But recently she's begun to feel just a bit lighter and seems to be bulging a bit more around the belly, or perhaps shrinking a bit around her hindquarters, and the lesion appears to be a bit larger. But even if I could corroborate these vague impressions, what would they mean about the progress or regress of her cancer, if that, in fact, is what she's got?

So, maybe I should stop checking on Phoebe all the time, just as I stopped taking my pulse all the time after I first recovered from my heart attack and triple bypass. It got so bad there for a while that I can remember myself continually fingering my left wrist with my right index finger, as if I were holding hands. And it certainly didn't improve my pulse any. As for the weather, it's gradually been clearing since about ten this morning, so the weather service isn't very far off, after all. Oh yes, there have been clouds up there, but so high, scattered, and thin that the day might be said to have fully recovered — all on its own.

TUESDAY / JANUARY 31

The last day of January, and in some respects it's ending much as it began. Bright sun. High scattered clouds. Several inches of snow on the ground. Sharply defined shadows angling across the snow. But the sun is higher than it was back then, and it's up almost an hour longer than it was back then. "The inexorable changes," as Kate calls them, are taking their course. Buds on the maple tree outside our bedroom window distinctly larger than they were at the beginning of January. Visible harbingers of spring more compelling by far than the fabled shadow of Punxsutawney Phil.

It's also much warmer today — upper thirties to low forties, rather than single digits to low teens, and only a light breeze now compared to a fifteen or twenty mile an hour wind back then. Much of the month, in fact, has been warmer than I expected given that first week of low temperatures and harsh windchills. So as I look out my office window at the Iowa River, I now see its dark green ripple from shore to shore, whereas it's often completely iced over right now.

Looking at my utility bill — almost fifty dollars less than last year — I'm tempted to be grateful for all those days in the upper twenties and lower thirties. The payoff has come not just in my checkbook but also in the rhythm of my life and the well-being of the plants. I've been able to walk to campus more often than usual, as I did for my class this morning. The trees and shrubs in the backyard have been subjected to fewer ice storms than usual. And the plants in the cellarway are more upbeat than usual. Rosemary flowering. Azalea forming buds. Sage putting out new leaves. Bay holding on to all of its leaves. Even the tropical lemon grass holding most of its green upper growth. All's right with the weather, at least for the time being. At this rate, the spinach will survive the winter, and maybe even the two artichoke plants.

But just when I'm savoring all these fruits of a warm January, I'm brought up short by the bitter taste of a *New York Times* report that "global warming resumed in 1994," that "the average temperature of the earth's surface rebounded in 1994 to the high levels of the 1980's, the warmest decade ever recorded," and that the rebound is reflected in the "exceptionally warm winter" we're currently having. And the fruits of this warmup can be seen not only in the floods of California but in the even more disastrous rainstorms now inundating Germany, France, Belgium, and the Netherlands. Some winter. I wish I could trade it in for an older model.

WEDNESDAY / FEBRUARY 1

It must be that I'm wedded to an ideal version of winter — a model of the season embodied in classical myth, English lit, and early twentieth-century weather statistics. A season that gradually works its way from the bitter cold of late December and early January to the first signs of warmth in late March and early April. From the illusion of death to the miracle of rebirth in ninety bracing days — give or take a few on either end. But now, it seems, I'm living through a postmodern winter with postmodern weather reporters. How else to account for their buoyant prediction last night of abnormally warm Marchlike temperatures in early February? Upbeat words and smiles all around, even though their anchor-buddies had just finished a glum-faced world-in-a-minute report about the worst floods in forty years inundating the Netherlands. As if there were no connection between global and local weather conditions. Tragicomic drama on TV news.

But why should I complain about the smiles of the anchor-groupies, when it really felt so good this morning to put Pip out on his leash and be greeted by the mild air and rising sun of an almost springlike day? So mild that even Phoebe headed for the back door without my having to put her out. And it wasn't just the feel of the air that buoyed my spirits. It was also the thought of being able to shed some of the heavy gear I've been wearing outside — the hooded parka over the pullover cap, the woolen mittens over woolen mittens, the walking boots over two layers of socks. And it wasn't just the anticipation, it was the walk itself, which turned out to be just as lightweight and airy as I thought it would be. So pleasurable I could feel myself smiling all the way down to the river — even when I slipped once or twice on a lingering patch of ice. So pleasurable I keenly felt the return to more normal conditions when I walked uptown to have lunch with Kate in the face of a cloudy sky, a bitter little wind, and temperatures that had dropped to the low thirties. Maybe I wouldn't have felt so bad about the drop had it not been for the beans and the greens, the potatoes and tomatoes in my salade niçoise that suddenly got me thinking at lunch about the spring and summer vegetable gardens.

Now that the weather is back to normal, I wish it had stayed abnormal a while longer. But when it was abnormal, just a few hours ago, I didn't know what to say (or how to feel) in response to the familiar question—"Isn't it a wonderful day?" I wanted to say, "Well, yes, it is splendid," but I also wanted to add in the very next breath, "I'm troubled by the realization that the warm weather we're having right now is inseparable from the recent flooding in California and the current flooding in Germany, France, Belgium, and the Netherlands." But I didn't want to rain on anyone's parade. And certainly not so fulsomely. So I kept my counsel and nodded ambiguously.

Is this what my younger colleagues mean when they speak about being "conflicted"? If so, it must be that I'm younger than I thought, and I don't like the feeling at all.

THURSDAY / FEBRUARY 2

All I need do to feel my age again is think about this morning's essay course, a favorite course that in one form or another I've been teaching for the past twenty-five years, and soon enough my thoughts are as overcast as this morning, especially when I realize that next year will probably be the last time that I ever teach it. Talk about weathering winter! There's nothing that makes me feel quite so chilly as thinking about the last time for this and the last time for that, with every passing essay. And the subject of this morning's piece, namely Orwell's "A Hanging"—about "the unspeakable wrongness of cutting a life short"—doesn't help any. Only our twenty-five-year-old cymbidium orchid that I brought up from the cellarway a few weeks ago can begin to sweeten my imagination.

Its long, green, straplike leaves rise up more than two feet and arch over like a fountain, producing a five-foot wingspread all around. Its multiple bloomstalks—some years as many as twelve, this year only seven—each produce fifteen to twenty small orchids. The first stalk started blooming this morning. So during the next two months, the plant will give us a show of about one hundred twenty little orchids. No one could ask more of a plant, especially given how little it's asked of us since we bought it in the early 1970s.

Kate occasionally saws it in quarters, repots the divisions, keeps one for us, and gives the rest away. Casting her orchids upon the waters, she invigorates our own. I feed and water it during its winter months in the cellarway and the house. But mostly this floriferous old cymbidium thrives on the weather that rains and shines upon it spring, summer, and fall, as it sits under the outer branches of the maple tree, taking in whatever comes its way. And it's shocked into forming bloomstalks by the extreme fluctuations in temperature that take place during the fall, when the daytime temperatures might be as high as seventy or eighty and the nighttime temperatures just a bit above freezing. So the abundance and beauty of its blossoms are truly a gift (and reflection) of the weather. More fluctuations in temperature, more bloomstalks and earlier blooms. Fewer fluctuations, as during this fall, fewer bloomstalks, later blooms, and paler petals, because they form during a period of limited daylight.

But even today, its pale mahogany petals and purple-speckled lips are vivid enough to remind me of the time, almost ten years ago, when Kate divided the plant while I was in the hospital after my heart attack, waiting for my restive heart to calm itself before a triple bypass. It was as if she did radical surgery on the cymbidium as a prayer, an offering, and a preparation for the surgery to be performed on me. And she cut well, judging from the continued well-being of the plant and of me. One of the cuttings she gave to my cardiologist, Ernie, an orchid fancier himself. And from Ernie I received not only my life but also two pink-flowering camelias a few years ago, a few hours after he died of cancer. But the climate of our house and backyard was clearly too hot and dry for them to bloom. So, I found them a home with Wayne, a former colleague and fellow gardener, who took them east with him this fall and recently sent me a photograph of them both, fully in bloom this winter. So many flowers from an old cymbidium on an overcast winter day.

FRIDAY / FEBRUARY 3

On an overcast winter day, there's also nothing quite like walking the ice-crusted, gravelly, asphalt alley that begins across the street from our house and ends on campus overlooking the river. The backyards look like February. Large patches of discolored grass, surrounded by dwindling sweeps of crusted snow. A rotary lawn mower sitting out the winter by the side of a garage. Diagonally across from the mower, a wire-enclosed compost heap, filled with pink grapefruit halves. A winterful of grapefruit. Then a fenced-in border collie, looking for action. A winterful of boredom. Then a rusting red wheelbarrow, wintering over on its side, in the middle of a backyard. Then the school playground, edged with dirt-covered snow. Snirt, as the locals call it. Snirt-covered ice lining the curbs. Heaps of snirt sitting around, like blackened permafrost. Detritus of winter. Further down, a bright green Christmas tree on its side, directly across from several transparent garbage bags, filled with dark brown oak leaves. A yellow broom leaning against a green doorway. A blue plastic bag dangling from the side of a black plastic wastebasket. And finally, just as I'm approaching the dorms, a young coed, her blond hair streaked with pink, red, and dark black strands, like the inside of an emperor tulip. Everything here just as it should be on an overcast February day.

Nothing is as it should be in the Netherlands, except for the tulips and the financial markets, both of which are outside the flooding area. Two hundred fifty thousand people homeless, but the flower people are happy to report that "the flooding will have no influence on the prices of tulips and bulbs." A spokesman for the country's dike agency predicts that Parliament will approve seven hundred million dollars for reinforcement projects. And the Amsterdam financial markets report that "stocks of companies involved in dike building rose sharply" this week. The more things change, the more they stay the same. The story of Kobe has now moved on to the financial pages, where the opinion is that "the colossal damage inflicted by the quake may take the shine off this year's opening months. But thereafter the colossal cost of reconstruction — with estimates running up to $70 billion and higher — will give an additional boost to economic activities in Japan and other Asian countries."

Everything, after all, running true to course on an overcast February day.

SATURDAY / FEBRUARY 4

"There's a winter storm on CNN News. A storm on CNN News." I was coming out of the shower this morning, when Kate relayed the news to me from downstairs — twice over, as usual, just to make sure I heard it right. She'd just finished talking to her sister, Martha, who had called from her home in Largo, Florida, a place on the gulf just outside of Tampa. I figured it must be a big deal, since Martha's somewhat like a fire alarm. She rings whenever there's a blaze in the neighborhood. This morning it was news of winds gusting up to fifty miles an hour, and a winter storm heading so far south it might freeze the houseplants on her terrace. The storm, she said, was part of a major one hitting the entire Northeast, predicted to drop eighteen to twenty-four inches.

Better a televised storm than no storm at all. So I turned on the TV, punched up CNN News, and got the tail end of a weather report about prodigious snowfalls around Boston and Connecticut. Then I switched to the Weather Channel and again got the end of a report about a major storm in the east, but nothing more specific. No pictures of falling snow, or drifting snow, or snow-clogged streets, or snow-stalled snowplows. Not even any exact measurements of snowfall, temperature, or windspeed. Just a weather map of the Northeast, with dark green and light green colors swirling over New York, Pennsylvania, and New England. A few more tries over the next few hours produced similarly tantalizing updates, but nothing specific enough to give me a clear idea of what was going on out there, much less a vicarious experience of the storm. Better an edible lunch than an invisible storm, so I made us one of my heart-healthy shredded cabbage salads with sliced red peppers, purple onions, and water-packed tuna, dressed in olive oil, lemon, mustard powder, salt, and ground black pepper. Crackers on the side, a bottle of tamari sauce to heighten the flavor, and chilled beer to top it off. Fortified for the afternoon, I decided to call some of my own contacts in the Northeast. First Trudy, a friend who winters in New Jersey (and summers in Wyoming), and the minute she started answering my question about the storm, I could tell from her bemused voice that the news was not quite what I expected. "Yes, we had about six inches overnight, but it stopped a few hours ago, and now it's just melting off the trees." Then my son, Marshall, who lives in Morrisonville, New

York, a little hillside town near Lake Champlain, where some of the heaviest snow was presumably falling. "Just three or four inches, Dad, and it's a dryish snow, falling slowly and gently, without any wind to speak of." Then as luck would have it, another friend, Jo Ann, called from Barrington, Rhode Island, about twenty miles from Providence, and her response was as puzzling as the others. "We had a lovely three-inch snowfall, but now it's turned to rain. The big snowfall will probably be in the upper elevations, in the Berkshires." After talking with Jo Ann, and checking the Weather Channel again, where a reporter was again talking about huge snowfalls on the way but mentioned only a few inches on the ground, I decided to call it quits. A false alarm, I thought. Or perhaps a slow-building snowstorm of major proportions.

The most definite and compelling weather, after all, was taking place in my own backyard, where a thirty-mile-an-hour wind had been howling in from the north all last night and all today, blowing out the overcast, bringing back the stars, blowing in a bitter cold front, bringing back the sun. If a wind that cold gets anywhere near Martha, it'll do in more than her houseplants.

SUNDAY / FEBRUARY 5

Last night the wind was still blowing so hard that Kate and I hailed a cab on the way home from the movies. The first time we've ever done something like that in Iowa City. Three dollars and twenty-five cents for a one-mile ride, but it felt so good to get out of the icy wind that I tipped the fellow a dollar. Not much to pay for escaping a windchill factor of twenty-four below. Not much to pay for Kate's momentary sensation of being in Manhattan again. The big city is only a cab ride away from your own back door.

This morning, though, the air was so calm and the sun so bright it was a pleasure to make my Sunday morning rounds to the recycling center and the co-op, especially given a relatively comfortable temperature of zero. Only zero—how easily we adjust to winter! A month ago, I was fretting about temperatures around zero. What would it take, I wonder, to make me adjust to twenty below? Or forty below? A season in the arctic? A course in cryonics?

And how about upstate New York and other places in the Northeast, where Marshall tells me the winds today are gusting up to fifty miles an hour, producing windchills between sixty and eighty below? Menacing for anyone, especially for people in the Northeast who've been having an almost springlike winter thus far. Nothing, I imagine, could adequately prepare one for such windchills. Still, the past two days have led me to ponder the idea of creating my own weather index, called a Winter Hardy Adjustment Table (WHAT, for short), designed to correlate duration of exposure to severe windchill, snowfall, ice, and other wintry conditions with levels of tolerance to such conditions, in order to produce an Overall Adjustment Factor (OAF, for short). I'm not very good at such calculations, but I bet my WHAT would show that a low OAF level produced the high level of excitement (and exaggeration) in some of those eastern seaboard weather reporters yesterday when they were describing the storm and predicting massive snowfalls. As it turns out, snowfalls ranged from six to eighteen inches. Not quite so prodigious as the predictions. But they were high enough — and the OAF level low enough — to disrupt travel throughout the Northeast, and to make life especially difficult and painful for the aged, the indigent, the homeless.

Only a snowman could be impassive in the face of such conditions, or someone who had been cold a long time — so long a time as not to feel the chill at all. I don't think I've ever known such a person, and don't think I'd ever want to, for fear of being frozen to death.

MONDAY / FEBRUARY 6

Such a crisp, clear midwinter day, it's a pleasure to be up and about, watching the birds from the kitchen window, checking the cymbidium to see if its second bloomstalk has started to open, touching up a few of my daily reports in the attic. Everything hunky-dory, until Kate reminds me of some unfinished business. "It's February and you still haven't finished your seed orders." And water the geraniums, I tell myself, before she goes up to the attic and discovers they're wilting in the morning sun. And take care of the white geraniums in our bedroom. And check the stuff in the outside cellarway. Once a command starts ringing in my head, others come rapidly to mind. And there's no way to silence them except to spend the morning putting things in order around the house. Midwinter guilt and expiation.

So I begin in the attic and work my way down to the basement. First, the ten untended geranium plants lined up along the window ledge right next to my computer in the east gable of the attic study, where I work on these reports every night. Why have I let those plants languish for two weeks, their pink flower heads and lower leaves gradually drying up before my very eyes? Kate, after all, goes to the trouble of trimming them, repotting them, and making plants from cuttings each fall, in order to save us the expense of buying new plants for the terrace each spring. Watering and turning them once a week is a minor chore by comparison. Much less trouble than having to clean up all their dead leaves and flower heads after they've gone untended for so long.

And the three white geranium plants by the south window of our bedroom. Why haven't I done anything for them during the past two weeks? Even now, it only takes a few minutes to pick off their dead leaves, prune the dried up branches, and water them.

And the vegetable seeds. Why haven't I finished ordering them, when it would only take an hour or two at the dining-room table to fill out the forms and order the leek plants, onion plants, starting mixes, row covers, and other accessories?

And the spider plant in the basement cellarway. Why haven't I watered it for the last several weeks? Or done anything about the last of the shrivelling plum tomatoes that I brought in from the garden back in November?

From attic to basement, my morning is like an extended guilt trip, with no relief in sight. Until I stumble on the tarragon plant that I pruned back to stubs last fall and have been watering each week and discover that it's just begun putting up new shoots since I last checked it. Never did I realize this aromatic herb had such therapeutic powers. One glance, one touch, and all my guilt was gone.

TUESDAY / FEBRUARY 7

Now all I need is an herb to diminish the bitter cold, especially the chills that come when I take Pip out for his evening constitutional. Pip would also appreciate such a magical herb, as I could tell last night, when the wind was so biting that he did his stuff and pulled to go back only a block from home. Back in time to hear David Letterman's Top

Ten answers to the question of the moment, “How do you know when it’s too damned cold?” A comic and raunchy routine, as usual, but none of Dave’s answers could equal Pip’s nonstop movement around the block, from tugging to squatting to tugging and back. With a dog like Pip, who needs a WHAT to measure his OAF?

And it wasn’t any better this morning, given a windchill of forty below. No wonder a female cardinal showed up at the feeder a half hour before sunrise and Pip was clawing at the door to get back in again just a minute after I put him out. Definitely a day to take the bus in rather than walk. And I’m glad I did. The two remaining blocks from the bus to the office left my hood-covered cheeks and my mitten-covered hands stinging with pain, long after I reached the building.

A quick check on my Internet weather sources brought me a special advisory from the Des Moines office of the National Weather Service, reporting that “an arctic front raced through the state very early this morning,” forecasting bitter windchills throughout the day, and advising folks “to wear the proper clothing so as to avoid frostbite.” Now it’s beginning to look like February’s below normal cold will more than make up for January’s above normal warmth.

Talk about a postmodern winter! And the power of El Niño too! What better evidence than months out of order? But no matter how scrambled the months have been, the seasonal patterns will inevitably assert themselves. The vernal equinox will come in less than six weeks, the first warm breath of spring soon after. And I intend to be ready for its embrace, as never before. So, before this bitterly cold day is over, I've resolved to plant my first vegetable seeds of the year. Seeds to produce a couple of patio tomato plants. I'll germinate them on the dining-room radiator, move the seedlings to the south window, and keep them there until the outside cellarway is warm enough to sustain them. Eight weeks from now, in early April, they'll be ready to spend their days potted up on the terrace. And seven weeks later in early June, if all goes according to plan, we'll have our first tomatoes — earlier than ever before. Cherry tomatoes juicy enough and piquant enough to taste almost like full-size fruits.

Come spring! Come tomatoes! Come summer in spring! And when it comes, the spring will seem so warm that all the world will be in love with it, and with that day, and pay no heed to summer!

WEDNESDAY / FEBRUARY 8

Summertime! Oh, summertime! The mere thought of it made me even more keenly aware of this morning's bitter cold. In fact, when I gazed at my little plastic pot of newly planted tomato seeds, covered with a bit of cellophane to hold in the heat and the moisture, it looked and felt like spring was very far behind. But the winter story for today is really unfolding in the Southeast. Arctic air bringing snow squalls to the Carolinas, below freezing temperatures and thirty-mile-an-hour winds to Atlanta, and freeze warnings to Florida. Warmer, of course, than it is up here, considered strictly in terms of the raw numbers, but probably just as cold — possibly even colder — for the people involved. A clear case in which it would be fascinating to study comparative OAF levels. But before any measurements are taken, I hope Martha takes her plants inside.

No matter how one measures the cold, there's nothing quite so warming as a bowl of homemade soup. Especially one made by Kate, who concocts them from her own fat-free broths out of everything from the garden and everything else that finds its way into the kitchen.

Beef bones, chicken backs, duck wings, fish heads, ham hocks, lamb hocks. Nothing escapes her soup pots, her fat skimmers, her strainers, her mashers, her blenders. And the result is a year-round procession of soups as varied as the weather. Gazpacho, minestrone, French onion, Russian beet, wild mushroom, potato and leek, tomato and tomatoes, cucumber and yoghurt. And don't forget the twelve vegetable soup. Also green pea, yellow pea, black bean, white bean, red bean, sixteen bean. And don't forget the lowly lentil.

But few have been quite so memorable as today's. A variation on the theme of Cuban black bean soup, but richer, denser, and more piquant by far than the familiar pitch-black purée. Maybe it was the mixture of her homemade broth and homemade tomato juice that made the difference. Or perhaps it was the battuto she concocted of cumin, oregano, dry mustard, minced garlic, ground cayenne, lemon juice, chopped tomato, and sautéed green pepper. But even the addition of that battuto to the simmering beans and broth could hardly have accounted for the meaty flavors arising from the bits of low-fat ham that she added to the broth and the simmering beans. And those bits of ham could hardly have produced the smoky taste that emanated from the minced pieces of defatted, parboiled ham hocks she added to the soup. And all those additions could not have produced the complex texture and taste that resulted from her puréeing some of the tender beans while leaving the others whole. Now as I sit here writing this report — the rich taste of that soup (that stew!) still lingering in my mouth — I can hardly wait for tomorrow's bowl, and the one after that, beans without end. Come to think of it, I wonder why I don't grow some black beans myself.

THURSDAY / FEBRUARY 9

Those black beans. They created such a storm inside me last night that I was awake off and on from midnight to morning, checking on the sky each time the storm arose. I saw the Big Dipper at one, watched the moon set behind the spruce trees at two-thirty, noticed scattered clouds moving in from the northwest around four, caught the first light of dawn at six-fifteen. And stayed up to watch it unfold, the stars disappearing as the light gradually increased, until only Jupiter was visible in the southern sky, and below it several bands of mauve-colored clouds, lightly edged in cream.

But the real show took place a few hours after sunset last night, when I saw a perfectly circular band of clouds or cloudlike stuff ringing the moon but not touching it. A halo so far out, in fact, it made the moon seem like the center of a bull's eye, or the iris of a heavenly eye, especially given the faint bit of haze immediately surrounding and touching the moon. But I couldn't immediately account for the perfect circularity of that outer band, that nimbus, so I called upstairs to Kate and phoned my colleague Paul, both of whom know far more about such heavenly phenomena than I. And just a few seconds apart each of them viewed the spectacle, and each surmised the halo was produced by the presence of ice crystals refracting the light of the moon. An icy eye. A mandala in the sky. As evanescent and haunting as the pale green light this morning.

Gifts of winter as fleeting as the sudden warmth of this day itself. Sunny, windless, in the mid thirties — the first day in February to come even close to its normal temperature. Brief respite from the arctic weather just past and the more severe arctic weather predicted for this weekend. A day just right for walking. Also just right for teaching E. B. White's "Once More to the Lake." An essay filled with so rich an array of summer weather — from the cool of early morning to the heat of afternoon to the relief of a late afternoon thunderstorm and the pleasure of swimming in the rain — that I almost forgot, as I always almost forget, how it suddenly ends with White feeling "the chill of death." But I didn't forget as I walked home in the chill air, looking over my shoulder at the fading technicolor sunset and a strand of pale green light.

FRIDAY / FEBRUARY 10

The spruces were up in arms this morning, their branches waving frantically, their sixty- to eighty-foot trunks swaying back and forth like a primeval chorus. And the big windows in the east gable moaning like so many windharps. Neither the sky nor anything else had actually fallen, but newspapers, oak leaves, plastic jugs, garbage lids, and branches descended on the back terrace and driveway as if from above. The wind blowing strong enough to create an afternoon chill factor of thirty below, and an evening chill of fifty-five below. Strong enough to provoke an all day "wind advisory" from the National Weather Service. "Motorists should exercise caution on Iowa roadways. People planning to be outdoors for any length of time should be dressed appropriately."

It's days like this that make me wonder about my attachment to winter, especially these stark winters on the edge of the Plains, where there's often no relief from the cold and the wind and the clouds and the freeze-dried grass, except for a few lingering patches of snirt. And even if there were a deep covering of snow, like the knee-high, waist-high drifts of my childhood, what would I make of it? I don't ski, don't own a snowblower, don't build snow forts anymore, don't do much with the snow except look at it, wish for more, and dream about being snowbound. So what do I get out of winter beyond its occasional gifts — a mandala in the sky, the glint of sunlight on newly fallen snow? Fool's gold. And even when I push the question, as I'm doing right now, I don't get much further than that age-old belief in the seasonal round. That commonplace notion that the exuberance of spring, the ecstasy of summer, and the mellowness of fall — all depend on the mortal cold of winter. As if winter exists primarily to endow the other seasons with their peculiar flavor. As if loss itself were all that made things precious. As if paradise were a bore, and everlasting spring or summer an intolerable condition. Well, it's a grand myth, especially for lyric poets and undergraduate English majors. I can remember how good I felt about the matter when I first discovered it in Shakespeare's sonnets and Keats's odes. But I can also remember the first time I saw native Hawaiians casting for fish and surfboarding along the windward side of Oahu, and I didn't see any signs of regret in their eyes for the absence of winter. No yearnings to exchange their lives for mine, certainly nothing to match my hunger right now to be back in Hanelei Bay with the sand under my feet, the sun on my cheek, Kate by my side, and the mild Pacific air all around me in a warm embrace. Some breezes, after all, are more comforting than others, no matter where you're standing.

❧ ❧

SATURDAY / FEBRUARY 11

Wind still blowing, windows still moaning, windchill still plunging, bringing birds galore to the feeders. Downy woodpecker at the suet cage. Sparrows, juncos, lady cardinal, male cardinal, blue jay, and red-bellied woodpecker all feeding together on the ground. No time for territorial pecking. Get your seed, get warm, and take cover. Red-bellied woodpecker so cold he's moved in from the fat feeder across the driveway to the seed feeder outside the kitchen window to the seed on the ground. Body moving sideways as if he were still spiraling up a tree. Head bent sideways as if he were still pecking suet from the cage. Too cold to figure out new ways of feeding. Get your seed, get warm, and take cover.

Cold as it is outside, the sun is high enough and warm enough to light up and heat up the windowsill on the south side of the dining room, where the newly sprouted tomato plants are spending their first full day above ground, just three and a half days after being planted. There's nothing quite like the gentle heat of a hot-water radiator emanating through a wooden sideboard to bring a seed to life. And nothing quite like the sun to bring a bit of color to a newly opened seedling. Yellowish this morning, their seed leaves turned light green by noon. So, on one of the harshest days of the winter the promise of summer is in the air.

And the lure of the tropics, too, especially around the three-tiered plant stand in the bay window. At the top of the stand a small jade tree, beginning to develop the bends and arches of a mature plant. On the tiers of the stand, a host of African violets, all blooming white. At the back of the stand, a wax plant winding its way up to the ceiling and down, covered with dark little flower buds beginning to expand. On the floor by the plant stand, six amaryllis pots beginning to send up stalks. On the sideboard along the east wall, a red poinsettia, its leaves gradually turning pale pink and green. Spirit of Christmas past. And by the east window of the dining room, the floriferous cymbidium, three more blossomstalks opening, urged on by Kate's daily mistings and the moistened air of the humidifier.

So many tropical plants — from the tomato of South America to the wax plant of Southeast Asia! But none so warming as the last bowl of black bean and ham soup.

SUNDAY / FEBRUARY 12

Everything so brittle and cold last night I could barely get the car plugged in to keep it from freezing. The receptacle end of the heavy plastic extension cord was ice-chilled from sitting on the back porch, so I had to bring it indoors for a few minutes to thaw it out on the living-room radiator before I could get the car plug to go into it.

Whenever the winter turns cold enough to freeze the electrical outlets, it's probably a sign that the psychological outlets have also been fouled up a bit. As I discovered this morning when I came home with the Sunday *Times*, a dozen eggs, a bunch of parsley, and an ecstatic announcement to Kate: "I just saw the car of my dreams in the supermarket parking lot." A faint smile crossed her face, a smile I'd not seen before in our thirty years together. And a strange invitation—"Tell me about it"—that I'd never heard from her before. As if she were the nurse in a psycho ward, and I were a loopy patient needing to be heard out. (But not so loopy that I couldn't manage to whip up her Sunday morning omelet.)

Actually, this whole car thing started a couple of Sundays ago, when Kate came back from taking her mother, Lib, to hear an organ concert in the old hometown church, twenty miles away, and returned with an announcement of her own: "You've got to do something about that car. The heater just doesn't work. We nearly froze coming back. Mother says you need to have the thermostat checked. And I agree."

But somehow between then and this morning, I forgot about getting the thermostat checked and starting checking into new cars. Well, not cars exactly. But sport utility vehicles. "Sport-utes," as they're called in the showrooms and car magazines. Actually, Kate had innocently aroused my desire for one several months ago when we were talking about our plans to travel more after I retire: "Wouldn't it be nice to have one of those four-wheel drives, so we can go out West and get up into the back country?" Just the sort of line that the rich, four-color brochures thrive on. Just the sort of line that echoed in my head this past week when I started visiting the Jeep and Isuzu showrooms, picking up brochures, and buying automotive consumer guides, to compare the merits and prices of rigs I couldn't possibly afford right now. "Cabin-fever-dream-time," she said, each time I came home with a new brochure or magazine. But I thought she too was interested, especially when she said that she too wanted the Jeep Grand Cherokee in "moss green." Now I don't know what to think, except it sure would be nice to have a heater that heats.

MONDAY / FEBRUARY 13

Up just in time to see the sun rising bright orange in the southeast horizon and a low band of clouds along the edge of the northwest horizon. The air so calm that nothing seemed to be moving in the backyard or in the sky. But forty minutes later, after breakfast and the morning paper, I noticed the sky was almost completely overcast. Those clouds that seemed fixed at the edge of the northwest horizon had actually been moving quite rapidly, driven I could then see by the upper-air current. So, it seemed, we were in for a cloudy day. Thirty minutes later, though, after a shower and shave, the sky had almost completely cleared again, leaving only a few scattered wisps along the edge of the southeast.

Cloudy then clear then cloudy then clear. As variable, uncertain, and difficult to interpret or predict as that lesion on Phoebe's hindquarters. Cancerous one visit, benign the next, then cancerous again. Six weeks ago, so gloomy a forecast, her demise seemed to be just over the horizon. This morning, a sunnier view. Yes, it's still cancerous, but her weight's holding, appetite's good, spirit's feisty — especially when the vet gives her an injection of cortisone. "She might hold on quite a while," she tells me, "especially given how well you're caring for her." I wonder whether she'd still think we're giving Phoebe such good care if she knew we're giving her that Ojibway tea remedy twice a day? I also wonder whether this member of the staff is just sunnier in her outlook than the one I saw last time. But then I remember that neither one of them was even willing to mention the dreaded "C" word until I brought it up myself.

Cloudy then clear then cloudy then clear. As variable, uncertain, and difficult to interpret as the Grand Cherokee thing with Kate. Yesterday, the bemused smile. Today at lunch, "how good it would be to have one of those Jeeps so we could go out West and get a better view of the full sky." The only problem is that after lunch, I went to the greenhouse to pick up something for Valentine's Day, and coming out I finally saw a Grand Cherokee in "moss green." And it wasn't at all the rich green color I thought it would be from the brochure. It was mossy—frog-colored but with a metallic sheen. And the molding along the lower half of the body wasn't dark black, as I thought it would be, but had a slightly silverish cast that didn't really go with the moss. Nothing, it seems, is what it seems to be, not even the moss green Cherokee.

TUESDAY / FEBRUARY 14

Thirteen above this morning—a balmy start by comparison with the last several days. A good omen for St. Valentine's. But when I put Pip out on his leash, the air must've hit me the wrong way because it suddenly felt intolerable. So cold, so harsh, I didn't even want to look at the sky or eyeball the backyard or anything else outside. I just wanted to get back in as fast as I could. And when I got back inside, something inside me almost screamed out what I was feeling just then in every part of my being. "I've had it. Had it with the cold, the wind, the ice, the ice-covered driveway, the ice pack over the backyard, the iced-over sidewalks, the iced-up car, my ice-nipped ears and toes and fingertips. And the heavy clothing. And the dry air. And the overheated rooms. Everything." Or words to that effect.

But Kate was still asleep. I didn't want to wake her up. And besides, the feeling passed so quickly I was left musing upon the suddenness of its appearance, as if out of nowhere. Like the dream I'd had just a few hours earlier about the end of the semester. It was the last week of classes, or perhaps exam week, or the week after graduation. No one around. And I was wandering the hallways, looking for someone to talk to, to have coffee with. But all the offices were shut. And no signs of light or life were visible in the gaps between the office doors and the floor. I was standing alone in an empty hallway, in an empty building. Not an uncommon experience when school is out. And sometimes, in fact, a pleasurable image to contemplate, especially in the midst of a semester when the press of students and committees becomes unbearable. But in my dream last night, I felt desolate beyond belief, with a great heaving in my chest. An anguish so intense I was on the verge of tears. And then I awoke, shaking. And then it gradually came to me that I must have been grieving the prospect of my retirement.

A strange twist, given the pleasure I've had this semester, on "phased-in retirement," teaching only one course with just a dozen students and a few auditors, who leave me almost completely free to write my daily reports and to contemplate the time when I'll be completely free to write, travel, and garden as I wish. I thought I'd adjusted to the chilly side of retirement, just as I thought I'd adjusted to the harshness of winter, except, of course, for a few qualms now and then, like the ones I had a couple of weeks ago. But when all is said and done, it must be that I'm troubled by a long run of bitterly cold weather, no matter where it occurs — wide awake or in a dream, in an empty hallway or right outside the back door. This winter watch is getting closer to home than I'd imagined.

WEDNESDAY / FEBRUARY 15

Every time the thirty-day forecast pops up on the Weather Channel, it predicts normal precipitation and temperatures for February. But February so far has been anything but normal. Virtually no precipitation other than a brief snow flurry several days ago and freezing drizzle last night. Below normal temperatures during the first half of the month, except for a couple of days near the beginning and a couple here in the middle. Temperatures in the mid fifties coming this weekend, as if it were April or May, rather than mid to late February. Does anyone at the Weather Channel bother to correlate the thirty-day forecasts with the daily or weekly predictions?

Or is February just a cockeyed month, unable to produce its "normal" temperatures in the low to mid thirties except by swinging between the extremes, between the teens and mid fifties? Sounds a bit strange, but the national weather map today makes the midsection of the country look like it's sandwiched between arctic weather throughout the north and tropical weather streaming into the south. And the state climatologist says this is the "time of year where we bounce back and forth between winter and spring."

It didn't feel at all bouncy when I took the garbage out to the compost last night or put Pip out on his leash. The skim of icy drizzle on the back porch nearly sent me skidding into the ice pack on the back terrace, and it wasn't any better this morning when I stepped out to get the morning newspaper, or when Kate went sliding on her way to the cancer clinic for a three-month checkup. Sky overcast and temperature hovering around thirty — just right to keep the skim of ice on the sidewalks. So I stayed home and transplanted the cherry tomato seedlings that had already started to put out their first pairs of true leaves. If the weather can bounce back and forth between winter and spring, so can I. By midafternoon, Kate had returned with a clean bill of health, and the sun itself had emerged, as if the day too had bounced from winter to spring.

Spring has also sprung in the center of the dining-room table, in the form of a dozen potted crocus — purple with orange stamens — that I picked up at a local nursery and brought home the evening before Valentine's Day. Six of them just freshly opened, others on the verge, all for just $3.75, compared to $5.00 for a single tired rose. Rose, thou art sick, thanks to the national florist syndicates.

But the real bounce in this household right now is coming from an orchid I brought home yesterday for my valentine (for less than a half-dozen roses). Its blooms long lasting, its roots tenacious, like hers. A robust *Phalaenopsis amabilis* with a two-foot stalk, topped by moth-shaped flowers four inches across — their petals and sepals pure white, their lips marked with coral streaks, yellow blush, and delicate hornlike appendages. It's sitting squarely on a pebble tray, but its flowers, suspended as if in midair, seem ready to fly away.

❧ ❧

THURSDAY / FEBRUARY 16

The full moon. It rose last night shortly before six-thirty and set this morning shortly after six-thirty. And as if to complete the symmetry, its point of arising was almost squarely centered at the back of our lot, right in the middle of the four spruces we planted some twenty years ago. And its line of descent was almost squarely centered at the front of our lot, right in the middle of the spruces the original owner planted a hundred years ago. How often, I wonder, do the orbits of our heavenly bodies seem to intersect so perfectly with our borders and our windbreaks, our landscapes and our lives? A good omen, I thought, especially because the sky conspired to be so clear as to provide a perfectly dark foil for the radiant light of the moon. So radiant it reflected vividly off the icy surface of the backyard, evening and morning alike.

But then, just as I was contemplating the significance of that omen, I turned on the Weather Channel and again heard about the abnormally warm weather predicted for this weekend. Possibly in the mid sixties. And then remembered that in February we normally have about ten inches of snow, but that virtually none has yet fallen. And then saw radar images of violent tropical storms, potentially tornadoes, moving from east Texas through northern Georgia and Alabama to North Carolina. Then I recalled the foot of snow that fell Sunday night in Portland, Oregon, the heaviest snowfall there during the last twenty-five years, a snowfall that could only have been produced by the rare intersection of frigid air from the northwest with tropical moisture from the south Pacific. And then I remembered the recent flooding in northern Europe and southern California. So much for the seemingly good omen of that picture perfect moon track! It couldn't hold a candle to the maniacal movements of El Niño. And as if to confirm its dire influence, my colleague David reported to me this morning that the central, southern, and eastern portions of Spain are in the midst of a severe drought — cracked ground, withered plants — and worse to come.

Just to make sure I wasn't making too much of recent divergences from modern averages, I consulted an illustrated medieval calendar in the *Très Riches Heures* of Jean, Duke of Berry — a French book of hours (for devotion and prayer) created around 1415. And there I found a picture of February — the only month with an overcast sky, the only one with snow completely covering the landscape. The only realistically detailed picture in the entire calendar. So, after all, I decided I should pay less attention to the orbit of the moon and more to the luny behavior of February 1995. Perhaps I should start the spring garden now, before the drought is upon us.

❧ ❧

FRIDAY / FEBRUARY 17

Omens be damned. What matters is the actual feel of things, and that's what got me this morning when I was standing on the back porch in my pajamas, the sun so bright I could feel its warmth on my right cheek. That touch of the sun drew me off the porch, across the snow-covered terrace, up the ice-covered steps to the row-covered herbs at the end of the gazebo—just to rub my fingers across the thyme and smell its dusky aroma on my fingertips. The first time since early January. And then to the main vegetable garden, just to rub some of the exposed soil through my fingers. The first time since late December.

That touch of the sun and the thyme and the soil—and the omnipresent sense of El Niño—also convinced me to start on the spring garden this weekend. So, before the weekend is over, I intend to plant up a few six-packs of broccoli, cauliflower, and lettuce seeds. Germinate them on the living-room radiator, move them into the outside cellarway under the Plexiglas, and bring them along until they're large enough and the soil's warm enough to transplant them outside under row covers. An early springtime replay of the late fall lettuce and radish routine.

That vision of an early spring garden also reminded me that I still hadn't yet called in my seed orders. So, this morning I went through the catalogue mail-order caper with all the cheery-voiced seed-order ladies from California to Maine. "Could you please give me your customer ID number, listed right above your name on the back of the catalogue?" Each time the cheery voice identified me as Kate Klaus, I said, "Well, no, not exactly," and each time the cheery voice blithely proceeded with the routine. "And which charge card do you plan to be using this morning?" "What is the number on your card?" "And the expiration date, please?" "And what is your first item number?" "And how many packets would you like to order of that item?" Seedtime on the telephone line.

That ritual preparation for spring drew me out to the riverbank below my office for the first time this winter. A midafternoon jaunt. The temperature so warm I didn't need a jacket. The sun so bright the river glistened like an impressionist painting. Dabs of light across a rippling green surface. And dried weeds waving along the edge of the shoreline. Pale wheat-colored tall grass. And red-stemmed branching stuff with curving wheatlike tips. And stiff grayish purple stuff with seed stalks top to bottom.

That touch of the sun and the wave of those weeds drew me to them as if they were long-stemmed flowers in midsummer — stuff just right for a winter bouquet of fall-dried weeds on an early springlike day.

SATURDAY / FEBRUARY 18

Springtime in February, chapter two. Mid fifties by midafternoon. Warm enough to be out in a lightweight farm jacket, taking stock of the trees and the shrubs and the raspberry beds. What a difference a week makes. Last week on this day the windchill was forty-five below. Today, a pair of young boys with a hardball and mitts are holding their first day of spring training in the street. As if the windchill were a thing of the past.

So is the snowcover — completely melted off the backyard by midafternoon. Swollen buds visible on all the trees, especially the apple. And the east side of the pussy willow opened again without any apparent loss from its premature show back in late December. Only a few rabbit-cropped stalks in the red raspberry patch bear witness to the cold and snowcover of the past six weeks.

If the temperature stays up in the forties and fifties, as it's predicted to do for the next few days, I can probably even seed in a row of radishes along the south side of the back vegetable bed and germinate them under row covers. Suddenly, it seems, I'm not feeling "conflicted" anymore about abnormally warm weather. Nothing like an arctic vector to help one get over such a conflict. And a realization that El Niño is with us to stay, like it or not.

Thanks to El Niño, I got to spend an hour or so with my neighbor Jim. We've been living back to back for twenty-five years now, visiting with each other in our adjoining yards spring, summer, and early fall. But when the fall turns cold, Jim's gone hunting, I'm gone teaching, and we don't get together again until the warm weather brings us back to our yards and gardens again. Today, as usual, I needed Jim's help getting something up higher than I'm willing to climb — in this case, a kestrel box twenty feet up on the mulberry tree at the back corner of the lot. Jim, as usual, was eager to help and full of lore about the creature in question. Though Jim's just a few years older than I, he's actually a hundred years wiser about wildlife. "I seen one on a fence post just last week. Out in the country. They got a red tail, buff red. Big wings, small body. Used to call 'em sparrow hawks when I was a kid. 'Cause they hunt sparrows. They also go after mice and baby rabbits and grasshoppers and moths. They dive straight down from midair. But you can also train 'em to eat outta your hand."

The kestrel box, as it happens, was given to me by Jean, a freelance writer who's auditing my essay class, after she heard me read my pieces about the winter bird survey. I also read them the one about the Grand Cherokee, but nothing moss green has yet shown up in the driveway.

❧ ❧

SUNDAY / FEBRUARY 19

The air last night was so calm and mild that I actually felt warm on the walk with Pip, and I was only wearing a lightweight jacket and gloves. But sometime later the wind turned around from southwest to northwest, so there's a little bite in the air, and it's not quite so warm today as yesterday. Only in the mid to upper forties. Only in the mid to upper forties! How quickly the extraordinary seems ordinary. Especially in this month of extraordinary gyrations and record readings. Temperatures so warm today from the Rockies to the Mississippi Valley that even the staid and restrained *New York Times* weather report announced that "record warmth will dominate the High Plains, the Rockies and the Southwest." And the cable weather lady echoes the

Times in her quick overview of the nation's weather: "It's hard to believe this is February."

But February it is, and the record temperatures are predicted to continue throughout the week. Last night's local TV weather reporter predicted highs in the upper forties to mid fifties continuing at least throughout Friday of this week. And this morning's *Times* affirms that "a wavy west-to-east jet stream pattern across North America will keep temperatures well above normal later this week and the weather rather dry." Only that last little phrase reminds me that this midwinter gift might ultimately come with a hefty price tag.

But it's hard to imagine the possibility of drought when flooding rains continue to fall across the Gulf States from east Texas to Florida, and water oozes to the surface under the branches of the maple tree outside our dining-room window, and puddles glisten on the lower level of the herb bed and the lower end of Kate's sixty-foot flower border, and the topsoil in the vegetable garden is so mushy with moisture that my foot sinks right into it as I'm trying to lift up the cover over the spinach row.

A quick peek is enough to show that the spinach has survived so well it might even kick in during the next few days. More and more motivation to seed up a few six packs of lettuce and other salad greens. So, I sterilize some of last year's starting mix in a 350-degree oven for an hour or so, let it cool down a bit on the kitchen counter, wet it up, fill a couple of six packs, and start planting viable seeds from last year and several years before.

Arugula, buttercrunch, Carmona butterhead, Tres Fin endive, Sinco escarole, Simpson Elite green leaf, red oakleaf, Medusa radicchio, Tall Tower romaine. A full range of colors and shapes and textures. Enough to create a gaudy display in the garden. And a gaudy array of succulent greens on the plate. "Like lips, like lettice," so a proverb went some five-hundred years ago.

As moist and tender and evanescent as the kiss of spring.

MONDAY / FEBRUARY 20

El Niño again. This time on the front page of the weekend edition of *USA Today*. The cover story, featuring a green-and-yellow-colored weather map of the United States, intersected by red, pink, and blue arrows, depicting normal and abnormal jet streams flowing over the northern and southern part of the continent. The gist of the piece is that everyone's talking about El Niño, even the characters in the TV drama *NYPD Blue*, because almost every part of the world has been affected by the "pesky pattern." From the flooding or abnormal warming in the United States and Europe to the drought and dry weather in southern Africa, Indonesia, and Australia.

I can't quarrel with the story. How could I, given all the fretting and fussing I've been doing about El Niño? But there's something about the piece that bothers me. At first, I think it's the breezy way it deals with the disastrous worldwide effects in a couple of brief paragraphs and then puffs up all the upbeat sides of the story in the United States — increased groundwater in California, easier harvesting and shipping of the corn crop in the Midwest, bigger snowfalls and a better ski season at Squaw Valley, bigger waves and better surfing in Hawaii.

But the more I think about the matter, the less troubled I am by the jaunty nationalistic angle of the story. *USA Today* is just doing its thing. And during the past few days, I'd have to admit that I too have been doing my own things to capitalize on El Niño. Still, it's difficult to keep thinking about El Niño without noticing the crazy-quilt distribution of its effects—flooding in France, drought in Spain. But then it occurs to me that El Niño may ultimately be no more irrational in its effects than the supposedly normal run of the weather.

Come to think of it, I wonder, what is normal weather? A recent study by a climate researcher at Princeton University suggests that "an irregular climate cycle" develops every sixteen to eighteen years, that other cycles cover longer and shorter spans, and that some of these cycles may influence or coincide with El Niño. So, El Niño may not be so strange or erratic or pesky after all. Just part of the wheel of natural fortune, like the seventeen-year locust. An upsweep or a downdraft, depending on how the wind is blowing.

Today it's been coming from the northwest at twenty-five to thirty-five miles an hour, which together with temperatures in the mid thirties to upper forties made me feel as if it were March rather than February, and that rather than walking down to school to write another report I'd much rather have spent the day in our neighborhood park just shooting the breeze or flying a kite. But walking back home, the wind was so fierce and the sun so far down that it felt like I was back in February again and El Niño was back in its box.

TUESDAY / FEBRUARY 21

"It's rosy out there." Actually, the rosiness was long gone, but Kate must have wakened long enough to see it out our south bedroom window, gone back to sleep, and wakened again with the color so vividly in her mind's eye that it might just as well have been rosy so far as she was concerned. The show itself — the gaudiest sunrise of the year — didn't last more than a few minutes or so, starting with a narrow band of amber fading into yellow, topped by a grayish purple layer of clouds. But then the amber and gray bands turned into an alternating sequence of rose and purple clouds, gradually radiating around the entire horizon.

Gradually changing from rose to peach to apricot. Gradually drawing me around the outside of the entire house in my pajamas, even though it was a chilly morning in the low twenties.

Just then, given the press of my wintery speculations, I couldn't help wondering whether the chill in the air and the strange sensation of being outside in my pajamas might have contributed anything to my pleasure in the sunrise. A squirrel-cagey sort of question that so often raises the hackles of Kate, it left me chuckling at what I imagined her saying if she'd been inside my head just then—"Why can't you just enjoy the sunrise as it is, without having to fuss over the experience?" And the chuckle came back again on my walk down to campus, when the air turned warmed enough for me to think about planting a few radishes outside this week, and then to ponder whether the pleasure of planting them would be heightened by the thought of doing so in the midst of winter, almost a month before the vernal equinox. Maybe this Niño-esque winter's not so bad after all, especially when it allows for such strange and unpredictable experiences.

Better still, tomorrow the temperature's supposed to move up again into the high forties or low fifties and stay there for the rest of the week. A haunting echo of this very same week in 1984, as I discovered from a gardening journal I started keeping back then on this very same day. Back then, it was fifty degrees "and higher temperatures promised for tomorrow." Back then, too, it had been warm "over the past week," so I could even begin to turn the soil I'd been unable to spade in the fall. And back then, I also noticed that the raspberry canes had been "eaten off with a sharp, diagonal edge about two feet above ground — a height that rabbits could easily have reached when the snow was new and hard in late December and early January." Maybe this winter's not so strange as it seems. I wish I'd kept up with that journal for more than six days, so I'd have some idea of how the rest of this bizarre season might turn out.

WEDNESDAY / FEBRUARY 22

Warm enough this morning for a full tour of the yard and gardens in my robe and pajamas. I just wanted to check the soil in the vegetable beds, take another peek at the spinach row, and see if the French chives or the parsley might be coming up in the herb beds. I also wanted to compare things today with my record of them eleven years ago.

Back then the parsley was "coming up in the center of last year's plants (the heavy snows must have fully insulated them)," the chives were "already emerging," and there was "a bright yellow goldfinch at the feeder." Today, the parsley was still green under the row covers, but the chives showed no signs of emerging, and a goldfinch was nowhere in sight, bright yellow or otherwise. Back then, too, the soil was not only warm enough to turn, but I was actually turning it. This morning, it was frozen from the overnight temperature in the low twenties, and it had already been turned in the fall by Dan, a graduate student who's been helping me do the heavy gardening jobs, now that my heart doctor frowns on the isometrics of handturning our clayey soil myself. The more things change, the more they're not the same.

But it could be worse, as I was reminded at lunch by my colleague Dixie, who greeted me with the memory of this day five years ago. "Can you believe this weather — in the fifties? Five years ago, the windchill was fifty below. Some difference, huh?" The thought of that hundred-degree reversal was almost enough to buoy me up for the rest of the day. It certainly did heighten the taste of my broiled salmon filet and chilled white wine.

I was also floating on a backyard conversation I had with Jim late yesterday afternoon. We were talking about the abnormally warm weather, and I was telling him how I'd like to get in some radishes and onion sets now, if the soil were just a bit dryer and warmer, when I suddenly remembered the vegetable plot that he has along the south end of his garage. A sun trap so warm that the tomato plants he grows there always bear fruit at least two weeks earlier than mine. We checked the soil, and it was way ahead of mine, almost ready to plant. So before the week is out, we've decided to work up that garden plot, seed it with a few rows of radishes, put in a few rows of onion sets if I can find them, warm up the bed with my polyester row covers, and split the produce. I can still hear Jim talking about the plan. "Just think of it. Radishes and green onions by the end of March or the beginning of April, when most years you're just getting 'em planted. Wouldn't that be something?"

THURSDAY / FEBRUARY 23

It sure would have been something, but it's not likely now — not after a twenty-mile-an-hour wind blew in from the north when I was walking down to campus and turned a temperature in the mid thirties into a windchill of twelve. And put me in just the right mood for this morning's discussion of Thomas's piece, "On Natural Death." I wish I'd worn my down-lined jacket, pulldown cap, and woolen mittens on top of my gloves. By the time I got down to the office, the cold wind was stinging my right hand, right cheek, and right ear — the parts of me facing the north — while the sun was warming my left hand, left cheek, and left ear. And when I took off my gloves, the difference was visible — pale, whitish tips on my right fingers, pinkish tips on my left. I felt as strangely divided as the Thanksgiving cactus in our north bedroom window, the right half of it covered with large coral-colored blossoms, the left side completely destitute of blooms and buds.

In this out-of-sync weather, everything seems to be at sixes and sevens, caught somewhere between early February and late March. Every morning, the garden soil is frozen stiff from the night before and the lawn feels crunchy underfoot, but by midafternoon the garden soil is oozing in the sun and the lawn feels firm but soft. On the north side of the house, patches of snow still linger on the grass, and the driveway is still covered with stretches of ice. On the south side, below the bay window of the dining room, daffodil leaves are an inch above the soil. And at the south edge of the terrace, the faint yellow tips of tulips have just broken through.

No wonder I'm torn between the yard and the house. Outside, I feel driven like a sleuth, like Sherlock Holmes in the garden, looking for every clue I can find that things are amiss, that the season is further along than it's supposed to be. All I need is my old houndstooth deerstalker and magnifying glass to complete the role. Inside, everything is immediately visible, asking only to be tended or admired, as if I were Holmes's Watson, ever eager to please. Move the tomato seedlings to the radiator every night and a sunny windowsill every morning. The same for the arugula, endive, escarole, and leaf lettuce, which have already started to emerge just four days after being planted. Water the cymbidium and phalaenopsis once a week. And behold them every day, facing each other on opposite sides of the living room, like yin and yang. The cymbidium — five of its bloomstalks almost fully open, arching up and over, a fountain of mahogany flowers. The phalaenopsis — five of its blooms fully open, a sixth just unfurling, a flock of pure white moths. No wonder I'm torn between the yard and the house. Seeking in one place, finding in another. Between two worlds, one on the verge, the other almost over the edge.

❧ ❧

FRIDAY / FEBRUARY 24

Back in '84 again, on a late-March–early-Aprilish day. Warm and sunny in the morning, overcast and chilly in the afternoon. Just like today, except then I was watching Arie, owner of Pleasant Valley Nursery, prune his way around the ten-year-old Montmorency cherry that Kate had given me for my birthday. I thought it only needed some heading back to encourage growth on its side branches, but Arie went deep into the center of the tree and gave me a lesson in the process. A lesson about fruit trees and the weather. I can still remember the twinge of pain I felt as he cut out its two largest vertical branches, the ones that gave the tree its distinctive pyramidal shape. I can still hear him laying down the rules in his friendly but firm Dutch accent. "Open up the center. Let the sun and air get inside. The best fruit comes on the laterals, out here, on the outer branches. On all fruit trees. All kinds." And I can still recall the bittersweet turn of his concluding announcement. "Not much fruit this summer. But more in years to come." And the tree lived up to his promise. Hardly any fruit that summer. Much more thereafter.

What he didn't predict was that the Montmorency would be dead just ten years later — victim of the flood of '93. And the apricot tree as well. Too much rain, too little sun, too many leaf drops, too many leafouts — all in one summer. And the European bird cherry too, a perfect bird-feeder tree, that used to stand at the top of the drive, off to the right of our kitchen window. Its trunk rent by a high wind the spring right after the flood, right before its regular May Day bloom period. All trees that Kate and I had planted, expecting we would all grow old together. Weathering the seasons together. Leafing and blossoming and fruiting down the years. And be survived by the spruces we planted at the back of the lot, the pin oak we planted at the end of the drive, the fringe tree and weeping hemlock we planted on the side of the front lot, the spindle trees we planted near the curb. Trees, after all, are the way we leave our mark on a landscape. And before we leave, the trees also mark the passing of the years, casting larger and larger shadows across the landscape. Talk about wintry thoughts!

But now as I look out the kitchen window, I see the dwarf Prairie Spy apple that I planted last spring where the May Day tree once blossomed. Just a whip of a thing, so small it can't hold a bird feeder, much less cast a respectable shadow on the drive. And looking out the back window, I can barely see the dwarf North Star cherry that I also planted last spring, standing a bit in front of where the Montmorency once reigned. No fruit from either tree this summer. Perhaps in years to come.

SATURDAY / FEBRUARY 25

Everybody's talking about the springlike temperatures, including me. And why not? Today was so warm—in the upper fifties to low sixties—I didn't even need a sweater. But how about the sun? Nobody's been talking about the astonishing show it's been putting on this month. Out and about for twenty-two consecutive days, during a period when it normally shines no more than fifty percent of the time. Oh yes, some days, like yesterday, the sun's been visible just half of the day and off duty the rest. And some days, it's been flickering on and off as rapidly as the moving clouds. But many of the days, like this one, it's been luminous from start to finish, as if it were July rather than February.

I've been paying special attention to it not only because of these reports but also because of my gardening. The green world, after all, is a gift of the sun. And when it disappears as it did for almost two months during the flood of '93, the harvest is grim. Dead fruit trees, shrivelled grapes, thwarted melon vines, rotting onions, diseased tomato plants, smutty corn. The rains contributed to those problems, of course, but the rain alone would not have been so damaging had it alternated with even brief periods of sunlight. Sometimes, I think the deepening depressiveness of that long dark summer could only have been cured by the long sunny fall that followed.

Sometimes, I also think I'm as heliotropic as a plant, dependent on sunlight for my own kind of photosynthesis — converting "all that's made to a green thought in a green shade." And sometimes, I just think I'm sun-starved because I spent most of my childhood years in an industrial, coal-darkened area of Cleveland. But Pip and Phoebe have never set foot in Cleveland, and they're as heliotropic as I am, especially in winter, each day moving from room to room, from bed to couch to rug to chair, to catch the rays of the sun. Just a few minutes ago, Phoebe moved herself to a window seat in the western gable of the attic to catch the rays of the setting sun. And now Kate is calling me downstairs to see it illuminating the white petals of the phalaenopsis.

On a sunny day last summer, Kate and I and Jim and our gardening friend Rebecca gathered together on our terrace shortly before noon to watch a solar eclipse. The newspapers, as usual, had ballyhooed it, diagrammed it, and given instructions about how to watch it safely with a handmade paper contraption. What they didn't tell us was that we could observe it just by watching the leaves cast thousands of crescent shadows on the flagstone — crescents that waned, then waxed, as the sun passed behind the moon. What they also didn't tell us was that during the eclipse everything around us, including ourselves, would seem to be at risk, especially at noon, when the light turned brassy, then dark, like gray glass, like black light, like darkness visible, and the breeze went dead, and the air turned chill, and all the birds fell silent.

SUNDAY / FEBRUARY 26

Kate's fifty-third birthday. And it began with a pithy report of her own, issued immediately upon arising. "Fifty-three. That's what it looks like. Gray and chill." And that's what it looked like all day long. Completely overcast without even a hint of the sun. Temperature just a bit above freezing from start to finish, and a mean little breeze, ten or fifteen miles an hour, for a windchill of only ten or fifteen above. Oh what a falling off from yesterday.

And nothing much better in store for the next several days. Arctic air moving in on the northern jet stream. March likely to begin as if it were early February or late January. If I didn't know any better, I'd hold myself responsible for breaking the magic run of sunny days and high temperatures. I never should have written about it yesterday. In the midst of an extraordinary run of good luck, I once believed, you were never supposed to talk about it, not even to utter a word about it, lest you break the magic spell. But maybe it was really Kate's fault. Just a few days ago, I can distinctly remember her saying, "I'm not ready for spring. I haven't had my fill of winter yet."

Or perhaps she brought it on by what she said about the sun last night after reading my report on it. "The sun is not a human personality. It doesn't come and go like you say it does. It only seems to, because that's the way we look at it from our perspective and the language that's built into us. It's just out there shining. All the time. And when we can't see it, the sun's not at fault, because the sun hasn't really disappeared. It's just that the clouds have come in front of it." Of course I agreed with her, because I know for a fact and from first-hand experience that she's right. For heliotropes like me, in fact, there's nothing quite like that moment in a long airplane ascent through heavy clouds when you break through the final layer of overcast and see the intense light of the sun, right there where it's always been, even though it may have seemed to disappear.

And yet there was something about her remarks that I couldn't quite agree with. That part where she said, "the sun's not at fault," or words to that effect, and then went on to say it was just the result of the clouds coming in front of it. What I wanted to say in response is that the formation of those clouds and the movement of those clouds is influenced by a whole bunch of things, one of which happens to be the sun. So, after all, the sun might be said to have a hand (even though it has no hands) in shaping the very forces that make it seem as if it's coming and going, appearing and disappearing.

But no matter how one looks at it, or words it, what I'm feeling right now is that I sure do wish the sky were not overcast, the sun were not hidden, the wind were not blowing, and the air were not chilling, so Jim and I could've gotten those radishes planted.

MONDAY / FEBRUARY 27

This one was supposed to be about my heart attack, because that's what I had ten years ago on the last Monday night in February—after a Chinese dinner of stir-fried pork, hot-and-sour bok choy, steamed rice, and fresh daikon radishes. Those daikon radishes were going to be a key image in the piece, or rather their burpy aftertaste, because as it turned out those rumblings were harbingers of the storm to follow. Gallows humor like that and clichés about weathering heart disease would be woven throughout the piece, along with wry comments and rhetorical questions, wondering why the weather got such a bad rap that it's associated with all kinds of trouble, from heart attacks to heartbreak. "Don't know why there's no sun up in the sky, stormy weather."

But just as I was puttering around in the kitchen this morning, pondering that line and others like it, Kate came down for breakfast with the cheery announcement that the tenth anniversary of my heart attack had passed into history a couple of nights ago, because, in fact, it took place ten years ago on February 25, the night before her birthday. But she hadn't said anything about the anniversary, because she was going along with my superstition about not talking about a run of good luck. "Do you remember what you said yesterday about not saying anything that might break a magic spell? Well, I've got a good piece of news for you." And so on.

Superstition be damned. Suddenly, I wasn't thinking about my heart attack any longer, but about our differing perceptions of when it took place. Or, to be more exact, about our differing perceptions of when the anniversary of it takes place. On February 25, the night before her birthday? Or on the last Monday night in February? Numerically, of course, she's right. And given her poignant point of view (as well as mine), there's no denying the fact that my heart attack came right after the dinner I'd made to celebrate the onset of her birthday. (Some birthday present!) But somehow, I've always also associated my heart attack with a Monday night, a night at the beginning of the workweek, a raw, cold winter night that sticks in my mind because those radishy burpings began right after I'd lugged three canisters of garbage down to the curb in time for the Tuesday morning pickup.

Now, I don't know any longer when the anniversary of my heart attack takes place. But I do know that I had one some ten years ago, give or take a day or two one way or the other, on a cold, overcast February day very, very much like this. And I also remember that a week later my cardiologist Ernie gave me a death sentence the likes of which I'd never heard before, when I asked him what would happen if I decided against his recommendation of a triple bypass—"You might live anywhere from six months to a year or two more, but I wouldn't give you much longer than that." Ten years ago I heard his chilly prognosis, and ever since then I've wondered about the arrival of winter—how suddenly and unpredictably it sometimes comes. So I don't plan to take the garbage down until tomorrow morning, and I don't plan to cook anything even remotely Chinese this evening.

❧ ❧

TUESDAY / FEBRUARY 28

On my way down to campus this morning, I was thinking how spring had disappeared and winter returned with a northwest wind, a dusting of snow, a clearing sky, and below freezing temperatures, when I was accosted by a man I'd never met before, never even seen before in my thirty-two years of walking around town. Six feet tall, full head of white hair, ruddy cheeks, cleanly shaven. Unzipped parka, folded newspaper under his arm, white shirt open at the collar. Black pants, black shoes, walking on the other side of the street. But the moment he saw me, he crossed the street, shook his head back and forth in a reproving gesture, delivered a weather report—"I told 'em summer wasn't here yet"—and kept on walking without breaking his gait.

I kept on walking too. Too stunned by the coincidence even to look back. But I couldn't help wondering whether he too was writing a winter book, or whether he was just playfully commenting on the return of cold weather in the mock tones of a smugly self-satisfied realist, or whether he had actually delivered a cautionary sermon somewhere, based on the abnormally warm weather. He looked like he could've been a minister in casual dress, heading for the entrance of the hospital I'd just passed.

The more I thought about his remark, the more I began to feel like one of his parishioners. Not that I'd ever thought it was summer. But last week sure had me thinking that spring was right around the corner, so much so that I'd wanted to go out and plant onion sets even before any of the local garden stores had them in stock. The desire was so strong in me that Kate had indulged it by picking up an expensive package of miniature cooking onions I could've planted had the weather not turned cold again on Sunday.

Maybe it's just that I have "receptors" for spring, as physiologists or ethologists might put it, so the combination of sunny days, warm breezes, and rising temperatures "released" an unalterable pattern of behavior, impelling me like the instincts of a wild creature to start planting things up. Even though I knew better — knew from the National Weather Service forecasts that arctic air was on the way, knew from the state climatologist's reports that despite the mild winter an early spring was not really in the cards, knew from my own experience that in this part of Iowa the ground never really warms up enough to start gardening outside before late March or early April.

But then again, I couldn't help thinking that I've always been pushing the weather. Always trying to do something early — all the way from skipping a year of grade school to phased-in early retirement. What's all the hurry about, I wonder, especially given what's left. Maybe, Kate's right. Maybe we haven't had enough of winter yet.

WEDNESDAY / MARCH 1

Does it come in like a lion and go out like a lamb, or come in like a lamb and go out like a lion? I used to think it was lions first, lambs last, but from year to year the order changes so often I'm not sure which one comes first anymore. And this year, just to make matters worse, it's neither roaring nor bleating so far. But it sure was bitterly cold last night when I took Pip out for a walk — the windchill then was ten or fifteen below. And this morning it was twenty-five below. This year, March is coming in like a polar bear, like January.

Talk about things being scrambled. In this Niñoesque winter, none of the months has been like itself, or the lore about itself, or the statistical profile of itself, or the predictions about itself. So, perhaps the best thing to do for the rest of this roguish season is to assume that the weather will deviate completely from the long-range patterns and predictions — in other words, that winter will continue to be as unpredictable as the weather. March is starting off bitterly cold and clear, when it was predicted to be cloudy and warm based on the thirty-year averages. So I assume it will wind up being warm and dry because it's predicted to end up being cold and snowy.

But no matter how it ends, I can hardly complain about the cold beginning, given the hearty pot of lamb shanks and lentils it called forth from Kate. A dish she's been refining since the first year of our marriage, when she discovered on a humid late-summer evening in 1967 that it's best served on a cold winter day like this. Since then, she's also discovered that rather than trying to bake those fatty, gristly limbs, it's best to poach them in a broth flavored with bay, celery, garlic, onion, parsley, pink peppercorns, black peppercorns, dried tomatoes, and alae (otherwise known as Hawaiian sea salt). A process that yields such tender meat it can easily be defatted, degristled, removed from the bone and returned to the strained, defatted broth along with the lentils, chopped onions, and some of last summer's canned tomatoes for the final marriage of meat and vegetables that produces this comforting dish. Together with a fresh spinach salad, sourdough bread, and a bottle of red wine, it's especially comforting on a bitterly cold winter night.

THURSDAY / MARCH 2

Last night, as it turns out, was actually the first night of spring, according to folks on the Weather Channel. Hard to believe, given the way things feel outside. But meteorologists, it seems, don't any longer reckon the seasons in terms of the solstices and equinoxes — December 21, March 21, and so on. Instead, they date winter from the beginning of December through the end of February, spring from the beginning of March through the end of May, and so on. So, today is the second day of spring. Not a very comforting notion, especially since everything in my body is telling me we're still locked in the grip of winter, with temperatures ranging from the single digits to the low twenties. And not only here in Iowa, but from Montana east to Maine and from Minnesota down to Missouri. Even if temperatures were in the mid thirties to low forties, where they should be right now, and the sun were shining, as it is right now, I still wouldn't feel as if it were spring. Something deep inside me would be saying, "it's still winter, still winter, no matter what they say." So what's going on here anyway? Who's got the real word on spring? When does it actually begin? For until I know when spring begins, how can I know when winter ends — and when to end this book.

I'd always thought that March 21 makes sense, because that's the date in the Northern Hemisphere when the length of day and night are almost equal. The vernal equinox. From then on, thanks to the tilt and orbit of the earth, the sun has more and more of an upper hand in all the things that mark the presence of spring. The flowering of squills, the crumbling of soil, the snake in the sun, the sweet aroma of growth in the air. The only problem is that here in eastern Iowa, March 21 is often so cold or snowy or icy that it doesn't really feel like spring.

I've also been consulting the poets and essayists to see how they detect the arrival of spring, especially because this morning's class is devoted to Hoagland's "Spring." But his fellow writers are not much help in resolving the problem. One thinks it approaches "sluggish dazed." Another that it "comes with a perhaps hand." Another that it arrives "deliberate and unabashed." Another that it's marked by "the spawning of toads." Another by "a tendency of man and dog to sit down somewhere in the sun." No wonder my colleague David once asked his writing students to propose various ways of determining the arrival of spring.

Just to add my two cents to the rest, I've decided to mark its arrival in my own fashion, in terms of the earth itself and whether it's ready to seed. So, I will henceforth consider spring to have arrived on that day when the air is warm enough and the soil is dry enough for me to draw my hoe easily through the garden, kneel down by the side of the furrow, and seed in a row of the first thing I usually plant — a row of Oregon Giant snow peas. Or this year, a row or two of radishes up by Jim's garage.

FRIDAY / MARCH 3

Spring hasn't yet come to the *New Yorker*, either. The issue for March 6 was sitting on the kitchen table when I got home yesterday, with a bleak, wintry, nighttime scene on the cover. Snow falling. Snow on the ground. Icicles on the roof and windowsills and entryway of a four-story walkup at the right edge of the picture. The rest of the picture dominated by the dark bluish gray superstructure of a bridge angling from left to right, with a snow-covered little hovel below it, two home-less people next to the hovel, warming their hands over a trash-can fire, and a dog standing in the snow in front of the trash can.

I couldn't help thinking of that scene when I took Pip out for his evening walk, not because it was snowing here—the snow is long gone. But because it was again very cold, and I had just come out of a very warm place with a very warm dog into a starry night so different from that graphic image of winter hardship in a faraway urban setting that it got me thinking again about the thousands of homeless people in Kobe. I was also set off by the glittering stars in the Big Dipper that had first got me thinking about Kobe when the quake occurred back in

January. It's a strange thing how the mind works, how one thing leads to another, and before you know it, you've gone from your backyard in Iowa City to a Japanese city thousands of miles away.

Suddenly, I found myself wondering whether Shizuko Hirajima had recovered any of her hearing after the shock of listening to her dying neighbors scream for help, and if Minoru Takasu had found a place to live after his home had been completely destroyed by the quake. And then it occurred to me I didn't know anything about how things have been going in Kobe, because Kobe had disappeared from the newspapers, even from the financial section of the *New York Times*, where it had last been celebrated as a hundred billion dollar boon to the economy not only of Japan but of all Southeast Asia.

Kobe was still on my mind this morning when I put Pip out on the back porch and the windchill was hovering around zero. And I thought about it again as I puttered around after breakfast, watering the lettuce seedlings and getting them comfortably situated on sunny windowsills in the dining room. What I couldn't get out of my head was a news photo several weeks ago of the Japanese empress clasping a homeless Kobe woman in her arms. A rare image, according to the *New York Times*, because the empress and emperor are untouchable. Also rare, because only such an image could have moved the story of Kobe back to the front pages of our country's newspapers.

According to my Internet weather maps, Kobe's daytime temperature yesterday was in the low forties. I wonder what it's like in the evening for those thousands of homeless people. I wonder what it's like for the empress.

❦ ❦

SATURDAY / MARCH 4

"Ordinary day? You must be kidding. It's a transitional day! Transitional! Everyone out here's scurrying around. Going to market. Laying in provisions. Putting down new bedding for the animals. Getting ready for the storm. It's transitional!" My friend Mary, who lives in a one-room country schoolhouse and writes about her rural life among the Amish, was trying to convince me that it wasn't just another sunny, uneventful day in early March. But at ten this morning, looking out at a clear blue sky without even the hint of a cloud in sight, it was difficult for me to get stirred up by her excitement. Oh yes, I'd tuned in to the Weather Channel and heard predictions of a storm, scheduled to arrive in midafternoon. But it looked like the brunt of it would hit the northwest portion of the state, and that here in southeast Iowa we'd probably get only an inch or two of snow at most (possibly in the form of freezing rain). Besides, I'd just been out to the compost heap, and the air felt so warm that I thought it might get up to the forties by midafternoon.

Just to be sure, I checked in with my colleague Paul, who's more of a weather bug than me. He's even got a special radio for continuous updates of state and regional weather. And he was almost as stirred up as Mary. "The worst of it will hit the northwest. But from what I've heard we're definitely in for it. I just hope we don't get the freezing rain again." He didn't call it "transitional," but from the way he was talking, it sounded as if he and Mary had the same sort of thing in mind. "It's sunny now, but just wait 'til this afternoon." Actually, I was more stirred up by Kate's special lunch of seafood chowder with clams, red snapper, diced potatoes, chopped onions, celery, bacon bits, and our own frozen corn. Together with the requisite saltines, her bread-and-butter pickles, and some chilled beer, it was a perfect transition between morning and afternoon.

Then Dan came over in early afternoon to rake up pine cones, branches, and other droppings from the spruces in the front yard, so that Kate's early spring bulbs would be able to get up without being stifled. Glory-of-the-snow, Siberian squill, and striped squill. And Dan also was muttering about the coming storm. Then Kate got in a few well-chosen words about the changing situation. "If you want to do something transitional, just go outside and help Dan rake away the winter and get ready for spring." By midafternoon when we were finished, the sky was clouding up and a little breeze was also blowing in.

So I decided to check the Weather Channel again, and the first thing I saw on the screen was a winter weather advisory. But the advisory had been moved from midafternoon to midevening, and the all-night storm had been cut back to a two-hour period at most, and the potential for a three-inch snow had been reduced to "accumulations of less than one inch."

Some transition. As transitions go, it couldn't compare to the one I saw right after sunset last night, when a thin band of orange light still glowed on the western horizon, and the sky above was turning navy blue, and the new moon glistened whitely with the old moon in its arms.

SUNDAY / MARCH 5

The long-awaited storm did finally begin to move in about ten-thirty last night, some eight hours after its scheduled appearance. The snow was just beginning to fall, in fact, when our local TV weather reporter took it to task for being "a slow-moving storm. Very slow." As if it were a sluggish worker or an overweight couch potato. Actually, it was quite industrious once it got here. And it dropped more than had been predicted in late afternoon. Three inches in three hours. A picture-book display. Dabs of snow strewn along all the branches of the deciduous trees. Cascades of snow weighing down all the evergreens. None of the freezing rain that had been feared or predicted. When it was almost finished around one in the morning, the landscape and trees were aglow with it, and we were almost lit up enough to go out for a snow walk, pajamas and nightgown be damned.

Six hours later, when I put Pip and Phoebe out, the snow seemed as fresh as if it had just fallen. Still clinging to the shrubs and trees as neatly as in the snow scenes of *Little Women*. Only a few paw prints visible in the backyard, none in the front yard, and only one pair of car tracks in the street. But just an hour later, when I went out to do my Sunday morning errands, it was already beginning to melt off the trees, soak into the ground, slush up in the street. A late winter storm. And now in late afternoon, none of it remains on any of the trees or in the street or under the spruces. And the ground is already showing in the gardens. Where are the snows of yesternight? Where are the snows of this morning?

This morning, the wet crunch of it under my boots immediately let loose the words of my childhood—"Just right for packing." And those words let loose the snowballs and snowmen of my Lake Erie childhood, when it was almost always just right for packing. Maybe that's why I was thinking of my Aunt Ada this morning, just before she called from Cleveland. Actually, she's not my aunt—she's my mother's first cousin—but she might just as well have been my aunt, given the weekends she lavished on me after my father and mother died. Now that Aunt Ada's ninety-three, her voice crackles so much I sometimes have to ask her to repeat herself. And she's so hard of hearing she often asks me to repeat myself too. "What did you say?" "What did you say?" Age has united us in a comic struggle to understand each other. But there are also moments when her hearing's so good and her voice so clear that she stymies me with questions in words as plain as day. "And what might be your motive for writing about winter?" I wish I had told her that I wanted to remember the important things in my life, like the snowstorm the night before that made me think of her right before she called. It was really just right for packing.

MONDAY / MARCH 6

Chilly and raw all day long, with another winter weather advisory for the entire state, predicting snowfalls up to ten inches before tomorrow and overnight winds gusting up to twenty-five miles an hour. Actually, the predictions started out rather modestly, with snowfalls projected between four and six inches, but as the morning wore on the predictions crept up a bit, elevating the blood pressure around here just a bit, what with Kate preparing to set off for a two-day indoor-outdoor tree conference a hundred and fifty miles west of here in Ames, Iowa. By the time she'd finished packing her suitcase and her carryall, as well as taking an afghan and a parka for safety precautions, she could easily have gone off for a week in the boundary waters area of northern Minnesota rather than two days in central Iowa. But she didn't want to take any chances, especially with Nancy in tow, an eighty-year-old cohort in Iowa City's Heritage Trees Program.

Kate and Nancy left in midafternoon, and since then I've been trying to make myself feel at home in this solitary place that's usually occupied by both of us in the late afternoons and evenings. Anymore, it's a rare occasion that either of us is away for more than two or three days a year. So whenever one of us goes out of town (and it's usually me), the other is left to deal with Pip and Phoebe fretting about the absent partner. Pip stood around this morning, anxiously watching Kate throughout the whole packing process. And Phoebe's been bellowing off and on, ever since she woke up from her afternoon nap and discovered that Kate had disappeared.

I've not been bellowing, but I sure do miss our nightly ritual of jointly planning and cooking a meal that we eat together at the dining-room table. Even though Kate had bought me a swordfish steak (one of my favorites) to broil for myself tonight, the companionship of Phoebe in the TV room, whining for morsels, left something to be desired. And Pip wasn't much better, hanging around for a few strands of my spaghettini with olive oil, garlic, and grated asiago. Only the sliced tomatoes were of no interest to him (and with good reason). An after-dinner stroll with Pip had something more to offer, especially since the wind had died down and a moist but grainy snow was falling. Faintly falling. And now as midnight approaches and I look out the darkened windows of the attic study at the entire sweep of the yard, I can see a new dusting of snow on all the bushes and all the trees from the yews right below to the spruces all the way at the back. The air itself luminous with snowlight.

But I'm haunted by a rabbit that hopped across the yard from our neighbor's some twenty minutes ago. A dark, solitary figure, hunched under the pear tree, directly under the bird feeder, dining on fallen seed. I'd like to sit here for awhile to see how long it stays, but I've a class to teach tomorrow and a soul to tend tonight.

TUESDAY / MARCH 7

Transitional. Ever since I heard Mary use that word to describe the day and the weather last Saturday, it's stuck in my head, because I've never heard it used that way before. I've usually thought of it as a word or phrase or sentence that connects one statement or paragraph to another. Or in music, as a passage that leads from one melodic line to another. Or in film, as a sound effect or voice-over or fade that leads from one scene to another. A bridge from here to there. Not very interesting in and of itself, unless you happen to be a transitionalist. Or a grammarian. Or a designer of bridges.

By analogy, I suppose that if you think of a day or part of a day or a bit of weather as being transitional, then it probably means you see it as being something like a bridge or a passage between one set of conditions and another. The calm before the storm. The dawn before the sunrise. The sunrise before the daylight? The lightning before the thunder? The thunder before the rain? The more I think about the matter, the more puzzled I become.

This morning, for example, when I first got up the sky was completely overcast, and it seemed as if the overcast would last all day, like the bitterly cold windchill. But an hour or so later, I noticed the sun was faintly visible in the southeastern sky, a sign that the cloud cover was probably a thin veil of moisture, likely to be blown away by the northwest winds that were then moving at about fifteen miles an hour. Was that thinly veiled sun a transitional point between the completely overcast sky and the fully visible sun an hour later? Or was it just a harbinger of a more genuine transitional moment I experienced on my walk down, when I suddenly noticed the snow at my feet beginning to brighten, turned around, looked up in the sky, and saw thin layers of clouds peeling away from the sun? Or was that striking moment just a prelude, a transition, to the veiling and unveiling of the sun that continued for the rest of my walk, as I could see from the alternating darkness and faintness of my shadow?

How can one possibly identify something as being transitional in a continually changing set of conditions such as the weather? And even if someone could establish a particular state of affairs as being transitional, who's to say what's more important? The transition? Or the conditions that precede and follow it? Or the transience of everything that exists? I used to think my phased-in retirement was just a transition between full-time teaching and full-time retirement. A way of easing out of one thing and into another. But the more I think about it, the more it feels like one of the most productive times in my life, as if everything else were a preparation for it. And it were all too brief, like life itself.

❦ ❦

WEDNESDAY / MARCH 8

So bitterly cold again this morning when I put Pip out that it felt like the first week in January rather than the first week in March, especially given the new snowcover from two nights ago and the ripples across its surface from the northwest wind that blew all night long, just as it did back then. In fact, the windchill this morning of twenty-seven below is exactly the same as it was on January fourth and fifth. The sky is completely clear just as it was on those days, so the shadows of the trees have been vividly cutting across the snow, much as they did back then. And the woodpeckers and starlings have once again been squabbling with each other at the fat feeder. If I didn't know any better, I'd say this was a virtual replica of early January, that we'd entered the twilight zone, and the year was replaying itself. Today, in fact, it's also going to start raining heavily again in California, just as it did in early January, with the likelihood again of heavy flooding.

Come to think of it, how do I know that it's not the beginning of January? How would I know if I didn't have a calendar and didn't have any of the modern media to tell me what's going on? I'd scan the book of nature rather than surfing the Internet. I'd see nature with my own eyes—unmediated by the media. I'd notice the swollen tree buds and the elevated position of the sun, which is markedly higher in the sky than it was two months ago and visible almost three hours longer than it was back then. And maybe I'd even notice that the shadows of the trees move at different angles across the snow. No wonder our ancestors were tree and sun worshippers. The elevation of the sun and the budding out of trees reveal the seasonal cycle's taking its inexorable course for all to see.

This day, after all, is like an open book, a paradox only on the face of it. Not like January at all, but like March. A month that's literally caught between winter and spring, and therefore always at sixes and sevens, lionlike at one moment, lamblike the next. Arctic one day, balmy the next. Bitterly cold today, temperatures in the sixties predicted for this weekend. Everywhere in the country, this month, whose name derives from Mars, is at war with itself. Conflicted. Thirty below in the Dakotas, not counting windchills, but high fifties along the east coast. Record snowfalls in upper Michigan, and heavy thunderstorms moving from Texas across the deep south to Florida.

In the midst of this warlike weatherscape, Kate has returned from two days of tree study in the arctic chill of Ames, bringing peace of mind to all the inhabitants of this household. No more bellowing from Phoebe. No more hangdog looks from Pip. And no more late-night meditations from me.

THURSDAY / MARCH 9

A whole clatter of display birds showed up for breakfast. Two jays, two pine siskins, two downy woodpeckers, a red-bellied woodpecker, a lady cardinal. And two redpolls quarreling in midair directly over the feeder, momentarily suspended as in an aerial pas de deux. Why didn't they schedule the Iowa Winter Bird Feeder Survey for today? But the real news this morning was the warmer, more tolerable air that I felt all the way down to campus. Probably because the wind was coming from the southeast rather than the northwest and only moving about five miles an hour. The sky was still clear at that point, but a few hours later when I went uptown to have lunch with Kate, the wind had picked up, and the sky had almost completely filled up with midlevel clouds — signs of the weather's gradually changing over from an arctic front to a warm front. And even if I hadn't checked the outdoor thermometers on the downtown bank buildings, I'd have been able to feel that the air was distinctly warmer after lunch than before. And warmer still by midafternoon.

So now the "S" word is on everyone's lips once again. Amy, a student in my essay course, was talking about it this morning. The local newspaper's all stirred up about it. And this afternoon, I overheard my colleague Paul announcing its imminent arrival to a prospective graduate student who had called him from New York. "Spring'll be here this weekend." Maybe, maybe not, depending on your perspective. But one thing for sure is that the irrepressible hunger for spring, for the weather to come, almost eclipsed today itself, almost turned it into a passageway, a transition, a conjunction. A mere "but" of a thing, as in "Yesterday, it was bitterly cold, but just wait until tomorrow."

Come to think of it, I'd been doing something like that myself, until all that talk about spring got me to thinking more just about this day, and not about anything to come. Then it was that I noticed the clouds breaking up a bit in late afternoon, gradually turning mauve then purple, as the sun, once again visible in the sky, turned the western horizon orange then amber in the course of its descent. A sunset worth seeing for no other reason than itself. So, I found myself thinking once again that it might be better to take things one day at a time. Sunrise to sunset, moonrise to moonset. No one could ask more of a single day.

FRIDAY / MARCH 10

When the sun starts rising, I rise too. It's not just that I'm a heliophile, but my eyes are sensitive to the first sign of daylight. So I've been waking a bit earlier ever since the winter solstice. And now that the sun begins rising about six-fifteen, I'm really beginning to notice the difference, as I usually do this time of year. Not only is my sleep cut short after six or seven hours, but I also find myself suddenly awake, looking for things to do. In a few weeks, this early rising will take me outside to plant and tend and inspect the vegetable beds. But for now, I'm still confined to the house, what with the ground still frozen or soggy or covered with snow. So after taking in a coral and pink sunrise, I took on all the lettuce and tomato seedlings that I started back in February.

The tomatoes, seeded in exactly a month ago and transplanted to four-packs in mid-February, had begun to get a bit leggy and root bound. So I moved them into deep, three-inch-square plastic containers, where they can spread out and develop roots all along their stems. Their next and final move will take place in late March or early April, when they go into large clay pots, to be set out on the terrace. Or they go up to Jim, since I've got three or four to spare. At this rate, we might even get tomatoes before my dream date of early June.

After the tomatoes, I took a breather on the back porch, where it was already above freezing and predicted to reach the mid fifties by afternoon. So I unplugged the heater in the lily pond, watched the snow melt off the gazebo roof, listened to the water trickle out of the downspouts, and tried to sniff the air for the aroma I associate with the advent of spring. But my nose was too stuffed to smell much of anything. And then back in for another bout of transplanting.

The lettuces, seeded in a bit more than two and a half weeks ago, were already so crowded and leggy that Kate was nudging me to "do something about them." The young lettuce seedlings always look a bit forlorn, probably because the warmth of the dining-room sills is not to their liking. So I reset the base of their leaves flush with the soil line, and now they look like proper little seedlings. Each alert, standing at attention. Even in this diminutive stage, the crisp, vertical Romaine is visibly different from the darker curly-edged endive, which is visibly different from the floppy, ruffly-edged Simpson leaf lettuce.

Then a brief soaking in water and SeaMix, a blend of kelp and ocean fish that not only nurtured the transplants but also transported me momentarily to the coast of Maine, where I first smelled the rank world of seaweed and sea life some thirty-five years ago. Some trip. And then I transported the lettuces to the outside cellarway, where they're probably feeling carried away even now by the cool moist air of that halfway house. The tomatoes will stay in the warmth of the upstairs a bit longer. To each its own weather.

SATURDAY / MARCH 11

Transplanting lettuces is always such a fussy job that when it's finished I breathe a sigh of relief, as I did yesterday morning. And this year, the job was done at exactly the time that I'm usually just beginning to seed up flats of lettuce. So I was also feeling pleased to be well ahead of schedule yesterday. But the more I've thought about being a month ahead with the lettuce, the more uneasy I've become about the possibility that this early lettuce crop might mature and begin to go bitter by the end of May. So now I'm faced with the prospect of having to start another crop right now, at the usual time, in order to have salad greens throughout the month of June and early July.

I've read about maintaining a continuous rotation of lettuce, but I've never done it, because I didn't want to get involved in the juggling of garden space and transplants that's required to bring it off. Mostly, I don't like the idea of being in two different places and two different times with one kind of vegetable. But here I am on the verge of doing just that without having foreseen it until just now. Only this year of scrambled weather could have tricked me into doing double time with the lettuces, and, come to think of it, with the patio cherry tomatoes too. For if I don't start another set of those seedlings now, the ones I transplanted yesterday will peter out by midsummer.

Talk about being scrambled by the weather, this week has gone so swiftly from one extreme to another — from bitter windchills a few days ago to mid sixties today — that it feels as if we've been in some kind of time machine. On Wednesday, I saw children in snowsuits playing at our neighborhood park, and at lunch this afternoon Kate looked out the kitchen window and saw someone flying a mylar kite in the park. "Can you believe it? Wednesday I was freezing in Ames and today I'm watching a kite in the park." Watching that kite, I could almost feel the tug of it in my hand, jumping and soaring high on the updrafts, swooping on the shifts of wind, as alive as a bluegill or bass, diving and turning on the end of a line. And the virtual feel of it took me back to the paper kites of my childhood, the ones I'd always get free in March and April whenever I went to the barber shop. From the barber shop, it was just a block to the schoolyard, where I'd unwrap it, put together the balsa wood struts, stretch the paper over them, tie up the string, run into the wind, and be launched into another world. Two places at once, all for the price of a haircut.

SUNDAY / MARCH 12

My prespring schedule calls for broccoli, cauliflower, and lettuce to be started indoors in mid-March, so I did it this morning right after breakfast. Comet and Packman broccoli, Cashmere cauliflower, and the same varieties of lettuce I started in February. A breeze compared to transplanting all those lettuce seedlings the other morning, except my mind was in two places and two times at once. At the kitchen counter with the seed packets, six-packs, and planting medium. And in the cardiac care unit at University Hospital, where I happened to be on this very same weekend ten years ago, getting ready for a triple bypass the first thing Monday morning. I remember that weekend not just because my life was on the line but because the weather back then was as abnormally springlike as it's been yesterday and today — sunny, breezy, with temperatures in the mid sixties. A bittersweet contrast to my own predicament, especially because I wanted more than anything in the world to be back home in my garden. Especially after Ernie, my cardiologist, stopped in to see me on his way out that Friday afternoon with the news that he was going home to work in his garden. By that point during my stay in his unit, he knew I was a compulsive vegetable gardener, as competitive about my gardening as he. So he knew that his parting words to me that afternoon — "I'm going home to plant lettuce, radishes, and peas" — were a taunt and a challenge. I told him his stuff would probably never come up, that it would almost certainly either rot in the cold and sodden ground or get nipped by a severe freeze before it could get established. I also told him that when I got out of the hospital I'd have my seedlings going before anything came up in his garden. And all my predictions came to pass. In fact, I had enough lettuce seedlings to give him some for his garden. Several years later when Ernie was dying of cancer and I visited him in the hospital, I wished there'd have been some taunt or challenge provocative enough to pull him through, just as his words that afternoon had helped to pull me through.

So Ernie was also on my mind this afternoon when I checked out that little sun trap of a garden off the south side of Jim's garage, the place where we agreed to put in a row or two of radishes for an early spring crop. It's not quite ready yet but certainly will be in a few days if the weather keeps up like this. I've never planted any vegetables outside this early, never before even considered the possibility of planting them this early, so I'm as eager to get in those radishes as Jim is to see whether we can attract a kestrel to that box he put up several weeks ago. Yesterday afternoon he was talking about it again. "I seen a crow lookin' it over the other day, but no sparrow hawk yet. Seen one out in the country though, just yesterday. Sittin' on a fence, lookin' down for things to catch. So I stopped 'n' looked at him, and he looked at me, and we just stood there like that for a few minutes, eyeballin' each other. Wouldn't it be somethin' to have one right up there?"

MONDAY / MARCH 13

Now that I'm on the verge of getting some seeds in the ground and some of my seedlings are taking the sun in the outside cellarway, it really does feel as if spring is in the air. Also as if the weather is even more compelling than it's already been, especially considering the shortage of moisture we've had so far this year. Forty percent of normal. A serious shortfall if it keeps up like this. Just like the way things started out during the drought of 1988. Right now we've got enough moisture from the flood of '93 and last year's normal rainfall to carry us for awhile. But the abnormally high temperatures of the past few days and the big winds all day Saturday and yesterday — gusting up to thirty-five miles an hour — could dry the ground out really fast. And then broccoli, cauliflower, and lettuce seedlings planted outside would be wilting in late April, just as they did back in '88. And I'd be watering the garden from May on. I sound like an alarmist. But the heat and the wind and the heavy air yesterday were unpleasant and unnerving, especially when the promised overnight rainfall brought only a fraction of an inch. And the temperatures are predicted to be twenty degrees above normal for the rest of the week, with little or no rain in sight. Jim says he talked to an old-timer out in the country yesterday, who thinks we're in for one of the driest summers in history. What an irony, given the deluge that's been inundating California once again the past several days. The worst this century. Bridges washed out, people drowned, homes flooded, crops destroyed, hillsides collapsing, highways cut off. So far as I can see, El Niño does no one any good.

Meanwhile, Kate and I are still debating what seeds to try out in our drought-threatened vegetable gardens. Though I've ordered all the new seeds, and they've all arrived, Kate keeps nudging me to consider some of the exotic things she runs across in the catalogues. Last Saturday night when I was cooking dinner, it was a Kishenev pepper from Moldavia and a Black Prince tomato from Irkutsk, Siberia. Nothing ordinary about those, especially the reddish brown interiors of the Black Prince. I'm always chary of tomatoes that come without any disease resistance, given all the diseases in our vegetable beds. But after a little go around, we settled on an Ecuadorian sweet relleno pepper and the Brandywine tomato, an Amish heirloom that several catalogues talk about as being perhaps "the best tasting tomato" they've ever grown. And before moving in on the pepper and tomato patch, she also got me to try a couple of oddball watermelons that she'd already ordered through the mail—Yellow Doll for its yellow flesh and Fun Baby for its telltale skin that turns yellow when it's ripe. "Can't you just let them roam around in some other crop, like the corn?" Well, it takes all kinds of vegetables (and compromises) to make a garden. I just wish some of their names weren't so creepy.

TUESDAY / MARCH 14

The weather's so wacky that it made the Late Night Show again last night. So warm that Letterman wondered whether "the earth has dropped out of its orbit and is falling into the sun." Seventy-one yesterday in New York City, the same in Iowa City. And the same predicted for today. But our state climatologist says not to worry. "If this were to happen a month from now in April, when we get temperatures 20 degrees above normal for a week, then we'd start worrying about what the summer is going to bring." So I'm not worrying. Not for the time being. Besides, it's hard to quarrel with the chives coming up in the herb bed, the daffodils poking through along the north lot line, the tomato seedlings now sunning themselves in the outside cellarway, as well as the colonies of snow crocus and snowdrops I saw on my way down to the office this breezeless mid-March morning.

Given my choice between last week and this week, I'd certainly take this one. Especially when I remember how my head was almost turned around by that arctic cold spell when Kate was away in Ames. That weather — and the time alone with Phoebe — had somehow gotten me to thinking so much about mortality that I'd worked myself into a dither about how we had to get all the things we wanted as soon as we possibly could. Seize the day, as they say. A trip to Europe, a return trip to Hawaii, a remodelled bathroom, and a moss green Cherokee — not necessarily in that order. Talk about cabin fever. I'd gotten so carried away that I even went to the bank to talk about refinancing the house so we could get all those things this year. And the banker, of course, completely agreed with me. "You only go around once," was the way he put it, "so we can arrange for anything you'd like." And when Kate came home, I was all primed to tell her how we only go around once and then give her a complete rundown of the plan and its financial advantages. But initially she was too tired, and later too busy getting her tree stuff put together, to hear me out. Actually, I now think she was just waiting me out, probably hoping I'd come to my senses on my own, without her having to help me along. And the warmup did, in fact, get me so absorbed in the garden and the seedlings and the swelling tree buds and the perennials pushing up that I gradually lost interest in that $50,000 refinancing package. Gradually realized, in fact, that my teaching schedule wouldn't leave us free enough to take either of those vacations or really make use of that Grand Cherokee. So as crazy as it seems, these abnormally warm temperatures have brought me to my senses, at the rate of a few thousand dollars saved for each degree above normal. What a difference a week makes, especially in March.

WEDNESDAY / MARCH 15

A perfect day for spring planting. Mid fifties this morning when I first went out to check on things in the backyard, mid sixties by lunchtime, mid seventies when I put my tools away in late afternoon. And the topsoil at Jim's was just right for seeding in the radishes. But when I got up to his place in late morning and was just about to cultivate his soil and rake it out for planting, something within me pulled back. Maybe because Jim wasn't home just then, and I didn't want to plant those radishes without making sure it was all right with him. Maybe because it was the ides of March, and I felt a bit creepy about starting a spring garden on so ominous a day. Maybe because I'd checked the *Organic Gardening Almanac* and discovered from the zodiac chart that March 15 isn't a good day for planting or transplanting root crops, but that March 16 is. Whatever the case, I got cold feet just when I was on the verge of breaking ground for the first time this year. And it didn't help when I found the soil at my place still just a bit too cool and moist for the onion sets I was planning to put in there today. So I decided to hold off until tomorrow, and not just to get another day of warmth in the ground, nor just to check in with Jim tonight. It also occurred to me that if I planted anything today, then this would be my first day of spring, and that would mean I should've ended the book yesterday, on the last day of winter. Besides, it seemed to me that I ought to provide a decent interval, a fitting transition, between the death of winter and the rebirth of spring.

So I decided to spend what was left of this day and the season doing some late-winter chores, like pruning the deadwood on the antique rose bushes and putting the raspberry beds in order. A day of tangles and brambles and emblems of the fierce struggle to survive that's been going on in the backyard all winter long without my having noticed it so clearly until today. First I cleaned up the red raspberry plants, deep-mulched last summer with well-rotted cow manure, only to find all of them cropped in half this winter by rabbits, probably during those beguiling January snows. Then the old rose bushes, surrounded by deer droppings and pruned back by the herd more severely than the raspberries. Looking at those raspberries and roses, I suddenly realized the winter had not been so mild as I'd thought, just because it had been cut short at both ends by the warming influence of El Niño. There'd also been those bitterly cold periods in January and February and again just last week, periods of great stress and risk for anyone or anything at the margins, as I had been ten years ago this week — my heart stilled, my body deeply chilled for the duration of that triple bypass. Winter, after all, even one as brief as this, does push us to the limits, and either we survive it or we do not. So even in the midst of lamenting those deer-bitten rose bushes and rabbit-pruned raspberry plants, I also felt a haunting sense of gratitude that Kate and I and Pip and Phoebe too had made it through another chilling time, especially when I found myself thinking about Shizuko Hirajima and Minoru Takasu, wondering what had become of them and all the other quake-ridden citizens of Kobe. So the spring planting I've planned for tomorrow will be conducted with a special hunger for rebirth both here and there. Radishes in the morning. Onions in the afternoon. And a sacramental glass of wine with dinner.

Summer Postscript

WEDNESDAY / JUNE 21

A week in the nineties, and the vegetables are so stressed out by the intense heat and lack of rain after the cooler and moister days of spring that I spent the morning soaking and mulching the tomatoes, peppers, eggplants, and squash. A laborious project that made me think about winter once again, with a longing for its cold embrace. And this afternoon, as if my wish were father to the touch, I found an update on Kobe in the *New York Times*, for the first time since early March. No mention of Mr. Takasu's fate. But Mrs. Hirajima, I learned, "has fixed up her home and moved back into it, giving up the tent in which she lived at first." Her two-story house, it seems, has became a one-story home as the result of a caved-in roof and the rebuilding process, but she didn't evidently have any complaints about that or her other quake-induced problem—"Recently my hearing got better, and now it's almost back to normal. There's no point in dwelling on the past. I've got to keep struggling ahead."

Though we've never talked, Mrs. Hirajima and I, her words are ringing in my ears right now and will, I hope, continue to do so whenever my winter comes.

BUR OAK BOOKS

Natural History

Birds of an Iowa Dooryard
By Althea R. Sherman

A Country So Full of Game: The Story of Wildlife in Iowa
By James J. Dinsmore

Fragile Giants: A Natural History of the Loess Hills
By Cornelia F. Mutel

Gardening in Iowa and Surrounding Areas
By Veronica Lorson Fowler

Iowa Birdlife
By Gladys Black

The Iowa Breeding Bird Atlas
By Laura Spess Jackson, Carol A. Thompson, and James J. Dinsmore

Landforms of Iowa
By Jean C. Prior

Land of the Fragile Giants:
Landscapes, Environments, and Peoples of the Loess Hills
Edited by Cornelia F. Mutel and Mary Swander

Okoboji Wetlands: A Lesson in Natural History
By Michael J. Lannoo

Parsnips in the Snow: Talks with Midwestern Gardeners
By Jane Anne Staw and Mary Swander

Prairies, Forests, and Wetlands:
The Restoration of Natural Landscape Communities in Iowa
By Janette R. Thompson

Restoring the Tallgrass Prairie:
An Illustrated Manual for Iowa and the Upper Midwest
By Shirley Shirley

Sarah's Seasons: An Amish Diary and Conversation
By Martha Moore Davis

The Vascular Plants of Iowa:
An Annotated Checklist and Natural History
By Lawrence J. Eilers and Dean M. Roosa

Weathering Winter: A Gardener's Daybook
By Carl H. Klaus